When You Fast

When You Fast

The Sacramental Character of Fasting

HAROLD RISTAU

Foreword by Thomas M. Winger

RESOURCE *Publications* • Eugene, Oregon

WHEN YOU FAST
The Sacramental Character of Fasting

Copyright © 2019 Harold Ristau. All rights reserved. Except for brief quotations in critical publications or reviews, no part of this book may be reproduced in any manner without prior written permission from the publisher. Write: Permissions, Wipf and Stock Publishers, 199 W. 8th Ave., Suite 3, Eugene, OR 97401.

Resource Publications
An Imprint of Wipf and Stock Publishers
199 W. 8th Ave., Suite 3
Eugene, OR 97401

www.wipfandstock.com

PAPERBACK ISBN: 978-1-5326-4879-3
HARDCOVER ISBN: 978-1-5326-4880-9
EBOOK ISBN: 978-1-5326-4881-6

Manufactured in the U.S.A.   MAY 13, 2019

Scripture quotations are from The Holy bible, English Standard Version® (ESV®), copyright © 2001 by Crossway, a publishing ministry of Good News Publishers. Used by permission. All rights reserved.

Dedicated to my gifted colleague and dear friend,
John Stephenson for his wisdom, devotion and faithful service
to our Lord's holy Church and her seminaries.

To Keep a True Lent

Is this a fast, to keep
                The larder lean,
                              And clean
From fat of veals and sheep?

Is it to quit the dish
                Of flesh, yet still
                              To fill
The platter high with fish?

Is it to fast an hour
                Or ragg'd to go,
                              Or show
A downcast look, and sour?

No: 'tis a fast to dole
                Thy sheaf of wheat
                              And meat
Unto the hungry soul.

It is to fast from strife,
                From old debate
                              And hate;
To circumcise thy life;

To show a heart grief-rent;
                To starve thy sin,
                              Not bin.
And that's to keep thy Lent.

—Robert Herrick, 1647, London

Contents

Foreword / ix
Abbreviations / xiii

    Prologue / 1
    Introduction / 6
1   Luther and Fasting / 12
2   Friend of the Ascetic / 27
3   Humbling the Soul / 42
4   Fasting and Prayer / 59
5   The Triadic Nature of Fasting, Prayer and Almsgiving / 68
6   The Evangelical Message of Fasting / 80
7   Fasting as Catechesis / 91
8   The Eucharistic Fast / 103
    Conclusion / 114
    Epilogue / 120

Appendix I / 131
Appendix II / 145
Appendix III / 161
Bibliography / 165

Foreword

THE AVERAGE LUTHERAN'S OPINION of fasting may be that it's merely an inadequate alternative to faith! This cynical perspective often arises from a garbled recollection of what Luther says about preparing to receive the Lord's Supper:

> Fasting and bodily preparation are certainly fine outward training. But that person is truly worthy and well prepared who has faith in these words: "Given and shed for you for the forgiveness of sins." (Small Catechism 5)

Luther's concern, of course, is the right use of the Lord's Supper; but his point could be applied equally to the right use of fasting. Just as eating the Sacrament of the Altar without faith is a mere outward observance, so also fasting merely in the flesh has no spiritual value. But when coupled with faith in the gifts to be received, fasting is indeed a "fine outward training."

This book is about the proper and profitable integration of body and soul, flesh and spirit, act and faith that ought to be second nature to sacramentally-minded Lutherans (not that there can be any other kind). Hence the thought-provoking title: The Sacramental Character of Fasting. One who understands Melanchthon's point in Apology XIII about the sacraments—that the precise number is a storm in a teacup, so long as one clings firmly to what Christ has given—ought to be open to the insight the title delivers.

The sacraments instituted by Christ unite Word and external sign in such a way that the grace of God is delivered through the body to the soul, and through the soul to the body, never one without the other. Ears, eyes, and mouth serve as vehicles for God's gifts. Faith has no access to God's spiritual goodness apart from physical means, whether in Word or sacrament. The sacraments instituted by Christ thereby reflect His very nature: just as Christ offered up His eternal sacrifice in both body and will, delivering His spirit to God even as His body expired and He breathed His last, so the sacraments unite the fleshly and the spiritual indivisibly. Luther, following St Paul's fundamental definition of the "mystery" (*sacramentum!*) as Christ Himself (Col 2:2; 1 Tim 3:16), boils it down to this: there is one Sacrament, Christ, delivered in three sacramental signs.

Dr Ristau contends that fasting be viewed through the same lens. Can fasting, coupled with the Word of God and faith, be a sacramental sign for the delivery of Jesus? Our Lord Himself does not allow fasting to stand on its own, but commends it along with prayer and charity (Matthew 6), thus laying down the classic threefold discipline of the church's penitential seasons. Fasting finds its meaning as it is interpreted alongside prayer (the soul turned towards God) and charity (the body turned towards the neighbour).

Denial of the body's desires serves the soul as it seeks to deepen and express repentance. Hence fasting isn't an end in itself but a tool in this spiritual discipline. Though most closely associated with Advent and Lent, to repent is simply to be a Christian. Fasting acts out the indissoluble connection between the acts of the body and the orientation of the soul. Denial of the pleasures of this world can thereby help turn the Christian towards God and His eternal goods.

The time is right for this book. Perhaps the time has always been right for fasting, but how much more in the modern Western world! Our culture is built on unfettered consumption and the pursuit of growth at all cost. Self-affirmation is an unquestioned virtue as the idol of self has supplanted the love of God and the neighbour. Fasting calls these worldly values into question and holds up the greater value of what God calls good.

Yet it is also true that the time is not always right for fasting. As repentance leads to forgiveness, fasting is meant to prepare for feasting. Advent leads to Christmas, and Lent prepares for Easter. The Christian who prepares through fasting and faith is well disposed to feast on the Lord's Supper to his joy and edification. Dr Ristau calls this the "dialectic" of fasting, and this dialectic has an eternal dimension. Even as this life involves a constant pendulum swing between repentance and restoration, fasting and feasting, so this life as a whole can be viewed as one gigantic fast aiming for the eternal and unrelenting feast of heaven.

This book cultivates such a perspective through appeal to the roots of our faith in Scripture, the Lutheran confessional writings, the wisdom of the Fathers, and the ceremonial traditions of the catholic church. It is eminently practical and down to earth, despite its heavenly goals. It has its feet planted firmly on the ground, in the personal experience of the author and the saints who have gone before. While the all-you-can-eat buffet may be the coarsest expression of the worldly consumerism that is the antithesis to fasting, such a cornucopia is indeed what this book offers. There is a morsel here for every reader seeking something to digest, albeit always in moderation!

I pray that this book's diet will nourish your spiritual discipline and draw you ever closer to Christ.

THOMAS M. WINGER, PRESIDENT
Concordia Lutheran Theological Seminary, St. Catharines, Ontario, Canada
Advent III, 2018

ABBREVIATIONS

AP   Apology of the Augsburg Confession (1531). In *The Book of Concord*. trans. ed. Theodore G. Tappert. Philadelphia: Fortress, 1959.

AC   The Augsburg Confession (1530). In *The Book of Concord*. trans. ed. Theodore G. Tappert. Philadelphia: Fortress, 1959.

AE   Luther's Works (American Edition). 55 vols. ed. Jaroslav Pelikan and Helmut T. Lehmann. Philadelphia: Muehlenberg and Fortress, and St. Louis: CPH, 1955-86.

SC   The Small Catechism (1529). In *The Book of Concord*. trans. ed. Theodore G. Tappert. Philadelphia: Fortress, 1959.

SA   The Smalcald Articles (1537). In *The Book of Concord*. trans. ed. Theodore G. Tappert. Philadelphia: Fortress, 1959.

LC   The Large Catechism (1529). In *The Book of Concord*. trans. ed. Theodore G. Tappert. Philadelphia: Fortress, 1959.

LSB   Lutheran Service Book. Prepared by The Commission on Worship of The Lutheran Church—Missouri Synod. Saint Louis: CPH, 2006.

LW   Lutheran Worship. St. Louis: CPH, 1982.

ABBREVIATIONS

NASB   New American Standard Bible. Michigan: Zondervan, 2002.

NIV   New International Version. Michigan: Zondervan, 2011.

TLH   The Lutheran Hymnal. The Evangelical Lutheran Synodical Conference of North America. Saint Louis: CPH, 1941.

Prologue

A Definition

CHRISTENDOM HAS NEVER CEASED to struggle for a conclusive definition of 'sacrament'. Broad definitions have often done injustice to sacred things. Narrow definitions have often prohibited us from fully appreciating those "pseudo-sacred" activities which are aspects of church life, but do not quite fall under any other doctrinal category. Even the early Reformers could not confess with complete certainty what activities were to be included as sacraments since the word itself does not occur in the sacred Scriptures, and so we should take care in our descriptions.[1] We Lutherans have wondered, "Are there two or three sacraments? Is the Office of the Ministry one? What about the fellowship and mutual support of believers?" The answer wasn't driven by legalism, but rather by an earnest desire to clarify the unique ways in which sinners receive the comfort of the Gospel. The categorizations of Roman Catholicism seemed to diminish the value of Holy Baptism, Holy Communion and the Office of preaching, by listing them among other rites that were not, strictly speaking, "means of grace". Martin Luther denies the seven Sacraments in his polemic against Roman Catholic theology in *The Babylonian Captivity of the Church* yet goes on to say, "if I were to speak according to the usage of the Scriptures, I should have only one single Sacrament, but with three sacramental signs".[2] In other words, as we hear in the First Letter to Timothy 3:16, Jesus Christ Himself is the chief *sacramentum*, in the words of the Latin Vulgate. The sacraments are unique modes of our

---

1. Chemnitz, *Examination of the Council of Trent II*, 23.
2. AE 36:18.

Lord's presence and unique vessels of the forgiveness of sins that He not only brings, but that He Himself is.

Likewise, the early Church was unclear on the matter since the Holy Scriptures described the concept in a vague sense, as a "μυστήριον θεοῦ" (i.e. mystery of God) which had a variety of usages.[3] The etymology of the word is itself a mystery.[4] The Roman Catholics have described the sacraments as "sign-mysteries" of the incarnation, the "abiding presence of the Logos" of which *the Church* as the body of Christ is the most comprehensive expression and thus, "the fundamental sacrament" from which all the others spring forth.[5] However rich such a definition appears at first, it cannot avoid robbing the two prime sacraments, Holy Baptism and the Lord's Supper, of their special quality. Perhaps we learn that attempting to take the mystery out of the *mysteries* by an exclusive definition is incongruent with the divine way. This by no means suggests that we discard our narrow and theologically priceless usage of the word which has its distinctive place in our belief and teaching but recognizes that it is not unorthodox to speak about sacraments in a broader sense, the way some other historic church bodies have.

For instance, because of their wider definition of sacrament, the Roman Catholics speak about things being "sacramental" and having a "sacramental character" as first articulated by St. Augustine. For them, these are theological terms which convey the idea that some things, like the soul, have indelible seals or marks imprinted upon them, "really and intrinsically present", which are produced by the sacraments. Because 'character' originally meant marks engraved on stone or metal as a symbol of ownership, they are basically the *markings* of Christian things and people. As a traditional Roman Catholic, Thomas Aquinas preferred to consider them as a quality inside the Christian soul having an instrumental power (e.g. a power to profess the faith). Accordingly, he argued that the Sacraments not only take away sin, but perfect the soul. They configure Christians to Christ as Head of the Mystical Body, setting them apart for Christian rites of worship according to "different degrees of participation in the priesthood of Christ". In the fourteenth century some understood "sacramental character" to mean "a relationship which God creates between Christ and

---

3. Elliott, *The Christ Life*, 13.
4. Kittel, *The Theological Dictionary of the New Testament* IV, 803.
5. *New Catholic Encyclopedia*, 786.

those receiving the sacraments".[6] The Roman Catholics are themselves not clear as to what they specifically confess. Often, we Lutherans are equally vague. Although the definition in this book does not accept the Roman Catholic understanding in its entirety, it admits that we can speak of "sacramental" as an adjective pertaining to other Christian activities which have a sacramental character, a divine quality about them as corollaries of church life in which the Sacraments are the foundation.

Struggling with the terminology, one could consider replacing 'sacramental' with 'mystical' or 'mysterious' to circumvent the problem. Yet all of these terms are equally ambiguous and problematic. And although they all convey a similar concept, only 'sacramental' denotes the activity as specifically Christian, only 'sacramental' is continuous with the historic Christian way of speaking, and only 'sacramental' allows us to think about fasting in a Christian way.

In support of this language, prominent nineteenth century Lutheran theologian Wilhelm Löhe described the Christian life as the Sacramental life which is "an experience possible only in the rich participation of the blessing of the sacraments".[7] Interestingly, he regarded himself as a "sacramental Lutheran". There is some leeway in our usage of the terms in question. Things can be sacramental in relation to the sacraments.

In short, there are lots of good reasons to get uptight. But sometimes we Lutherans do it for the wrong reasons. In our righteous zeal for preserving the uniqueness of the sacraments of Holy Baptism, the Holy Supper, and the Holy Office of the Keys—in their common function of delivering the Gospel of the forgiveness of sins, rescuing us from death and the devil and offering us salvation—we leave little room for speaking about those precious Christian practices that do not qualify: how to talk about the mysterious or "sacramental" character of marriage or the preparation for death, or the blessing of objects and the treatment of "sacramentals". Speaking about other activities as sacramental does not need to undermine the primacy of the means of God's grace to the Christian Faith.

Adopting a broader definition of sacrament deepens our appreciation for the sacraments proper, by including relations with Christian activities such as fasting—things which, as you will see, are a familiar part of the

---

6. *New Catholic Encyclopedia*, 786-787.
7. Deinzer, *Wilhelm Löhe's Leben* II, 523.

daily Christian walk.[8] My intentionally inconclusive definition[9] which best encompasses the Christian spirit of 'sacrament' (as opposed to '*the* sacraments') has been adopted from John H. Elliott, *The Christ Life*, which describes it as "the mysterious communication of divine things . . . sacred things which God uses to shape us, shape and determine a person's whole character and style of life".[10] He continues by calling Sacraments

> spaceless, illocal places where God meets us with the Gospel and mysteriously and mystically transforms us into his image. Thus, there is a *sacramental character to many Christian activities, anything that serves the Gospel and increases our faith* . . . .Of primary importance is the fact that the sacraments are channels of the grace of God and exhibitions of the Gospel (italics mine).[11]

The idea is that the sacraments have a kind of bipolar nature as they are both actions of God and actions of the believing community,[12] insofar

---

8. Liturgically, one could say the same thing about the preparatory rite of Corporate Confession and Absolution to the Service of the Word and Service of the Sacrament during the divine liturgy. Although the "entrance rite" is not, properly speaking, part of the Divine Service but a later addition, the Church has included it in, and has thereby enhanced the significance of what follows. Mostly everything that happens during the sacred church service is, in a sense, sacramental, due to its relationship with the sacraments.

9. In his helpful book, *The Christ Life*, John H. Elliott challenges us to widen our understanding: "One of the hermeneutical benefits of a broader definition is that traditional definitions concentrate so exclusively on the objective 'what' of the sacraments that they fail to communicate adequately today the 'why' and 'wherefore', that is, the manner in which the sacraments affect and change people" (Elliott, *The Christ Life*, 10). Yet "what if they actually are meant to be appreciated not as things or objects for study but rather as actions and signs of a relationship between God and man and his fellowman? What if they are ways in which Christians celebrate relations with God and to their neighbor? What if they are real 'happenings' by which Christians give thanks for the grace and love of God which happens to them all over the place? What if they are [also] signs of a dramatic acting-out of all the experiences of life: birth, life itself, death, sorrow, friendship? What if sacraments are not [merely] remote and ancient ceremonies but rather celebrations which effect character and attitude and give a person a new understanding of himself?" (Elliott, *The Christ Life*, 8). "This all suggests that the sacraments are not [merely] 'things' or 'objects' but actions; the action of God and the reaction of God's people. The sacraments are not static: they are sacred happenings." (Elliott, *The Christ Life*, 17). The sacraments are the occasion of the dynamic self-revelation and effect of the creator God within his creation (Elliott, *The Christ Life*, 72). Therefore, they are the "totality of God's saving action and of the Church's believing response" (Elliott, *The Christ Life*, 13).

10. Elliott, *The Christ Life*, 13, 7.

11. Ibid., 15.

12. Ibid., 17.

as the person is the receiver of God's redeeming and sanctifying works. Because fasting is an act of man and does not forgive sins, it surely is not a sacrament "in the same way in which Baptism and Lord's Supper are truly and properly" sacramental.[13] Yet, again, there is a way of talking about the sacramental character of fasting, by virtue of its connection to the sacraments (in particular, the Sacrament of the altar) without confusing it with the sacraments proper, which uniquely offer the forgiveness of sins, in a visible way, and as clearly dictated by the Word of God. After all, as we will see, fasting 'sort of' has God's command, is 'sort of' visible, and certainly *prepares* one for God's forgiveness. Because something divine, timeless and life-changing is received and communicated through fasting as it stands in relation to the sacraments, it can be described as having a sacramental character.

---

13. Chemnitz, *Examination of the Council of Trent II*, 23.

Introduction

I AM TERRIBLE AT fasting. On those rare days when I choose to forego my lunch, it doesn't take long before my mind becomes preoccupied totally with suppertime. It doesn't put me in a better mood either. Nevertheless, if we learned that most of our attempts at Christian piety demonstrate not how well we do them, but how poorly, we would probably be farther ahead in our spiritual race. Yet that doesn't mean that we ought not keep trying. And by the end of this book, I am hoping to have made some sense from that statement.

In recent years, due to a new appreciation of numerous medical benefits, the secular world has expressed a renewed interest in fasting.[1] But this is not the sort of fasting that we will explore here. Christian fasting is of a different sort, practiced for different reasons. Unfortunately, the topic has been neglected by most Lutherans who consider it at best an educational exercise and at worst, outdated and destructive to faith. However, as Richard Foster points out in *The Celebration of Discipline*:

> Why has the giving of money, for example, been unquestionably recognized as an element in Christian devotion and fasting so disputed? Certainly, we have as much, if not more, evidence from the Bible for fasting as we have for giving. Perhaps in our affluent society fasting involves a far larger sacrifice than the giving of money.[2]

Although this statement may be a little harsh, it exposes the unfortunate fact that fasting has been all but entirely forgotten by Christians who treat it as outdated and unimportant. This is largely due to the fact that its role in the Christian life has been misunderstood. Its function within church

---

1. Towns, *Fasting for Spiritual Breakthrough*, 180.
2. Foster, *Celebration of Discipline*, 47.

INTRODUCTION

life has been ignored. By delving into the Holy Scripture, tradition, and patristics, both pre- and post-Reformation, I hope to demonstrate not merely its importance, but also to unveil a surprisingly sacramental quality which pastors and laity alike will find edifying in their devotional lives.

Fasting has no sacramental character in itself. It is the function that it serves within the economy of God's forgiveness and His means of grace which gives it this character. Insofar as it relates to the sacraments proper and serves their unifying agent, absolution, it is sacramental. Fasting includes a relationship to confession and repentance, and to that for which it longs and prepares, absolution, culminating in the Eucharist. Each chapter of this book operates within the parameters of this dialectic, demonstrating its usefulness in the believer's life as it celebrates the many workings of our God who hears our cries, answers our prayer, transfigures our hearts, and uses our hands and mouths to bring His transforming power to this helpless and broken world.[3]

Because of what it offers us and effects in us, fasting's sacramental character, once grasped, motivates Christians to fast for reasons belonging not to the realm of Law but to that of the Gospel. We do it, not because we absolutely must, nor because we probably should, but, because we cannot help but do it. Like many aspects of the sanctified life, we have less choice in this matter than we think we do. After all, we belong to Him and not ourselves. And that's a good thing.

Because of this sacramental character, Christian fasting can be distinguished from the fasting of other people groups. Some have fasted purely as a form of asceticism. Others have observed it as a penitential practice towards purifying the self or atoning for sins and wrong doings. Most religions designate certain days or seasons as times of fasting for their adherents, such as Yom Kippur for the Jews, Ramadan for the Muslims, and the Day of Humiliation and Prayer for Christians. Certain events in the lives of individual persons have been designated as the most appropriate times for fasting, such as the day or night before a major personal commitment. The vigil of knighthood is a historical instance of this practice.[4]

For the Christian however, fasting—the practice of abstaining from activities—normally from food, either completely or partially, for a specified

---

3. The Epilogue and Appendices are intended as resources to pastors for congregational use.

4. Towns, *Fasting for Spiritual Breakthrough*, 174.

period[5], is done for a variety of reasons and motivations contingent upon specific contexts[6] and reflected in the various usages of the word and synonymous notions uncovered in the Scriptures. The common Hebrew translation for the word 'fast' is "abstaining from food" or "to eat no bread" (1 Sam 28:20) an idiom reflected in Luke 7:33.[7] Yet the Hebrew phrase "to bow down one's soul" (Lev 16:29) conveys the idea of "afflicting oneself"/ "afflicting body and soul" (Isa 58:3,5) and "humbling oneself". Such expressions conveying the notion of "self-denial" are closer to the original meaning. According to an older expression in the Pentateuch it is "to do violence to the natural life",[8] to "press", "to tie up", or "to constrain" the flesh for spiritual reasons. The idea of "mortification", though unpalatable to Christians who boast a "prosperity Gospel" that values temporal pleasure above eternal promises, is also an appropriate Biblical description.[9] Mortification conveys a natural and physical expression of grief often connected with the mourning process, and which naturally flows into prayers of penitence. The Greek text similarly refers to fasting as a self-mortifying humbling [Col 2:18 reads "humiliation of mind", echoing the Semitic periphrasis "affliction of one's soul"[10]]. But νῆστις more generally means "one who has not eaten, who is empty"[11] or one who "is unsatisfied". It can also mean generally "to be hungry, without food" (Mt 4:2, 6:16 ff; Mark 2:18; Luke 18:12; Acts 13:2),[12] inculcating the general sense of "not having eaten", "being without nourishment", and even "*suffering* hunger" and has thus been included in the list of the apostles' sufferings (2 Cor: 6:5,11:27).[13]

It sounds rather masochistic, doesn't it? Indeed—unless we recognize that fasting, like all self-mortifying acts of Christian piety, are not to be valued as ends unto themselves. It was St. Augustine who clarified the nature of an idol by making the helpful distinction between the two hermeneutical concepts of "use" and "enjoyment"; that all things have good and bad uses. They are misused when they are "enjoyed" as principles unto themselves,

---

5. Ibid.
6. Freedman, *Anchor Bible Dictionary*, 775.
7. Ibid., 773.
8. Delitzsch, *The Prophecies of Isaiah*, 385.
9. Leupold, *Exposition of Isaiah*, 286.
10. Freedman, *Anchor Bible Dictionary*, 773.
11. Kittel, *Theological Dictionary of the New Testament*, 924.
12. Ibid., 925.
13. Ibid.

instead of as "useful" in servitude to God. When we set things up as ends in themselves, we inadvertently create an idol, a competitor to the one true God who alone is to be "enjoyed" as an end in Himself. In terms of fasting, our attitude towards fasting and reasons for doing it, is the principal way of determining its value. Just like any good work, it may be good in itself, but it can quickly lose its goodness when the motivation of the one who does it becomes impure or self-serving. So, although some Church Fathers viewed fasting as a virtue containing an intrinsic goodness in and of itself, others, such as St. Augustine, treated fasting not as end unto itself saying: "that God only approved of fasting if it brought us back to [other] ultimate ends."[14] Though what that ultimate end is may sometimes remain a matter for debate, most would agree that it is intended, in some sense, for the worship of God. This is indeed the "use" of fasting since in God alone are our souls at rest (Ps 62). One of the most popular Russian mystics, St. Serafim of Sarov (1759-1833) argued that *all* Christian asceticism should be aimed at the acquisition of the Holy Spirit, "whereas prayer, vigil, fasting, and other Christian practices however good they are in themselves . . . serve only as necessary means for achieving it."[15]

In fact, fasting is a means of maintaining a correct and Godly order to the elements of which the self is comprised. A balanced self results in a peaceful spirit. All consumption outside of moderation is abusive. We become enslaved to idols that seek our misery and destruction. In this sense, gluttony does not just involve overeating, but consuming things outside of their rightful order. Another word for this is "abuse" which can take on many forms. Thomas Aquinas argued that gluttony

> denotes a disordered desire for eating. This disorder must be seen with regard to the food that one eats, as well as to the eating of this food. With respect to the former, a person can manifest a disordered desire for food in three ways: first, by seeking costly or luxurious foods; second, by preparing foods with excessive effort; and third, by consuming food in excessive amounts. As for the eater himself, gluttony is manifested in two ways: in the mode of one's eating (in eating too quickly, at the wrong times, and when one is not hungry; in being impatient to eat while awaiting its preparation) and in the manner of one's eating (namely, without observing due propriety and restrain in one's consumption).[16]

14. Reijnen, *Fasting – Some Protestant Remarks*, 275.
15. Jones, *The Study of Spirituality*, 270.
16. Loughlin, *Thomas Aquinas and the importance of fasting to the Christian life*, 353.

A healthy self-identity insists upon a moderation of all things useful. A deformed self, by overuse of God's gifts, has thus misused them. The use of tools for purposes for which they were not designed, usually results in injury. I tried to use a brick one time to hammer in a nail. It was a bad idea. I smashed my thumb instead. Tools can be friends or foes depending on their rightful use. In the spiritual realm, the consequences are more grave. In Plato's *Republic*

> the decline of the human person's character and morality is seen in the person of the tyrant as he throws off the right ordering of his nature, allowing his appetites to exercise a rule that reason ought to exert... when the virtue of temperance is missing, people's affective nature, no longer integrated into the whole of their humanity, begins to manifest itself in deformed way... The glutton displays a loquaciousness not befitting the temperate person.[17]

Fasting is never an end but is a means of more fully appreciating heavenly things. Hence it is always connected to and accompanied by other activities such as private and public repentance and confession of sin; *ascesis* and spiritual warfare; humiliation, lamentation and mourning; prayer and almsgiving; teaching, evangelism and liturgy; worship and in preparation for divine communication. Just as a written document produces various meanings for those who read it, so does the exercise of fasting for those who practice it.[18] Although many non-Christians fast for individualistic reasons driven by health or dietary concerns or as an attempt at moral or spiritual progress, Christians see fasting from a more global perspective. It is a tool aimed to remind not just themselves, but the world around them about our common desperate spiritual condition which leads us to repentance:

> In light of what has been said, the practice of fasting undertaken apart from a moral or a spiritual context appears as little more than the voluntary imposition of pain and suffering (through self-denial of the very substance required for one's physical well-being) for the sake of one's health (for example, to lose weight, to reduce one's blood pressure or cholesterol, to relieve lower back pain, etc.), one's appearance (to achieve a better self-image, being able to fit into a dress or a suit, etc.), or at most one's mind, namely, that it be free for greater application to one's studies (by reducing the body's involvement in the processes of digestion so

---

17. Ibid., 354.

18. Adalbert de Vogüé, *The Rule of Saint Benedict: Doctrinal and Spiritual Commentary*, 234.

that one's energies might partly or wholly be turned to contemplation). When viewed, however, within a Christian context, fasting becomes an implicit recognition, and a personal declaration to oneself and to the world ... [of] a being that has a choice of comporting itself either to the world below or to the one above, or resting either in the pleasures of this world or in those found in God himself.[19]

So little respectable material has been written on the topic in the last few hundred years that the present-day application of the topic is in many respects a venture into unexplored terrain. Most of this other literature seeks to answer the questions, "what can *I get out* of fasting? *How long* will it take to get it? What must *I do*?" Yet this line of questioning, emerging from a vain heart, is the wrong one to pursue. True fasting is less a work of man and more a gift of God. Through a historical study of the role that fasting has played in the Church from antiquity—and seasoned with a few personal anecdotes and reflections—I hope to come closer to answering the difficult question posed by many Christians today, "Why fast?"

---

19. Loughlin, *Thomas Aquinas and the importance of fasting to the Christian life*, 357.

1

LUTHER AND FASTING

CHRISTIANS TODAY MIGHT BE surprised to hear how the great sixteenth century reformer, Dr. Martin Luther, talks about fasting. He says more than we would expect. There are well over fifty citations in his work. The majority of his references however are negative, serving as reactions to the unhealthy fasting that Luther was exposed to as a monk. Understandably, he is constantly warning Christians to avoid turning fasting into an act of works righteousness, namely, doing it for the wrong reason. In the *Apology* of the *Book of Concord*, the Lutheran reply to the *Roman Confutation* which rejected many of the key efforts at reform in the Medieval Church, Philip Melanchthon criticizes human reason which persuades us to view fasting as a rite that justifies. For instance, Thomas Aquinas in *Summa Theologica* expressed that "fasting avails to destroy and prevent guilt",[1] and African theologian and polemicist Tertullian (160-220) stated that fasting is a "sacrifice which reconciles God".[2] A false understanding of the purpose of fasting abounded in many of the writings of the Church Fathers. Yet there were

---

1. AP: XV.

2. Kittel, *Theological Dictionary of the New Testament*, 934. Incidentally, this sort of piety was not unique to Christianity but was also present in Rabbinic Judaism. Rabbi Eleazar says "fasting makes a saint", that it "expiates sin", and that the power of change lies in good works (Kittel, *Theological Dictionary of the New Testament*, 931). This early Jewish attitude towards fasting which included "atoning for involuntary sins" is based on Leviticus 4 and 5 and is echoed in the *Song of Solomon* (Ps Sol 3:8)(Wimmer, *Fasting in the New Testament*, 12).

as many who would have agreed with Luther's assessment and his zeal for centralizing Christian life around Christ's righteousness and not our own. The Lord accepts our fasting, not on the ground of our righteousness but on the ground of His mercy.

Commenting on doctrines of works righteousness that also penetrated Luther's personal monastic experience, he says,

> Fasting has become a means of seeking great merit before God, of atoning for sin, and of reconciling God; in absolution, therefore, they have imposed this fasting as an act of penance.[3]

Luther wonders whether or not fasting as 'satisfaction' is intended to satisfy God or man; i.e. inflate our egos. Clearly, "by piety and fasting we crucified Christ by dropping out justification."[4] Luther is not opposed to fasting, but to trusting in fasting as a work of righteousness. In his commentary on St. Paul's letter to the Galatians in 1535, he writes: "We today do not reject fasting and other pious practices as something damnable, but we do teach that by these practices we do not obtain forgiveness of sins."[5] Elsewhere he states: "But on no account dare it be done for the purpose of making it an act of worship or a means of meriting something and reconciling God."[6] After all, the "prophet Zechariah (Zech 7:5;8:19) rebukes the ungodly prophets who wanted to attribute their deliverance to their own endeavors like fasts and not to the promises of God."[7] We encounter this same disgust in the words of the Prophet Isaiah in chapter 58, where he rebukes false fasting, the sort of fasting which is undertaken as a duty, instead of as an expression of faith, and produces an ill-tempered, irritable community.[8] Because the fasting of these Israelites was not motivated by love, the affliction they experienced, in a sense, caused them to afflict others. When undertaken for the wrong reasons, fasting does not even produce works that appear righteous, but rather ones that are clearly evil. Isaiah would have agreed with the suggestion made by St. Augustine (354-430) that abstaining from "strife and discord" is a true fast.[9] It is as ironic today as it was then that the strictest

---

3. AE 21: 158.
4. AE 54: 338.
5. AE 26: 84.
6. AE 21: 159.
7. AE 17:158.
8. Delitzsch, *The Prophecies of Isaiah*, 386.
9. Augustine, *Sermons on Liturgical Seasons*, 85. [for a complete exegesis see appendix I]

fasters are often the worst hypocrites. In the words of Luther in his *Table Talk*, "the most pious monk is the worst scoundrel",[10] because, as renowned hermit and Western scholar St. Jerome (348-420) wisely observes, "fasting provokes pride, pride which is the enemy of God."[11]

Instead, Luther writes, "The Father does not love us because of good works or fasting, but because of belief in Christ, that is what pleases him."[12] God loves us despite ourselves and despite our good deeds which aren't that good, but are actually "filthy rags" (Isa 64:6) in comparison with Christ in whom "a single work excels the works of all men".[13] In a *Sermon of the Gospel of St. John* Luther states that

> God's justification is free and unmerited, and so our hearts must cling to him and turn from [this kind of] fasting, and serve Christ alone, aside and apart from our work, so that we may be justified.[14]

And in his *Catholic Epistles* he writes that "we may weaken and mortify the body with fasting and work but "*we* do not expel evil in this way!"[15] It is God, not we, who effects spiritual things, even though God may choose to act in response to our fasting.

Surrounded by the legalism of the Church at that time which led Christians to believe that they were righteous before God based on their works rather than Christ's, Luther carefully reformed the Church ensuring that he by no means and under no circumstances create new laws and thereby cheapen the precious Gospel. The early Lutherans despised the mandatory fasts that the Papists created as they "burdened consciences."[16] Laws and rules pertaining to the fasts of the Church seasons continue in the Roman Catholic Church today, although any enforcements have been lightened by ecclesiastical leadership in the last few decades. Yet when made mandatory, such fasts must be rejected since they lead God's people to trust in themselves rather than in God for salvation. "A *necessary service* of fasts

---

10. AE 54: 340.
11. St Jerome, *Letters*, 256.
12. Ibid., 234.
13. AE 26: 182.
14. AE 23: 24.
15. AE 30: 41.
16. AC: XXVI.

on prescribed days and with specified foods confuses consciences"[17](italics mine) and is thus to be abolished, as are any and every *man-made command*:

> prayer, charity and fasting have *God's command* and where they do, it is a sin to omit them. But where they are not commanded by God's law but have a set form derived from human tradition, such works belong to the human traditions of which Christ says (in Matt. 15.9), "In vain do they worship me with the precepts of men." Thus certain fasts were instituted not to control the flesh but, as Scotus says, "to pay homage to God and to compensate for eternal death."[18] (italics mine)

The numerous Medieval Catholic rules regarding fasting and traditions of fasts of which Luther is so critical were spiritually unbearable for the struggling Christian who took his piety seriously. As Luther sarcastically states in his commentary on the Sermon on the Mount,

> from the Jews we took over our great season of fasting in Lent. At first we kept fourteen days, too; but then we became holier and stretched it out to four weeks, and then finally extended it to forty days. But even that was not enough, so that as additional fast days we set aside two days of every week throughout the year, Friday and Saturday. Finally, there were the four golden fasts or compulsory fasts. Now, all these were only the general fasts. Over and above them, Advent found some special saints of its own, who made it into a fast. On top of this, there were the monastic observances in the monasteries and the particular saints that everyone selected in excess of the general fasts.[19]

Now Luther is a little hasty in his judgement here. For instance, one of the earliest of Christian documents describing Christian practice, *The Didache*, indicates that biweekly fasts on Wednesday and Fridays was a common Christian practice in the early Church. Yet Luther's point is well taken. The underlying reason for this unbalanced emphasis on these days of fasting was human pride. A "good" Christian faithfully following this arbitrary fasting calendar could simply put a mental check mark beside the days on the list whenever a fast was fulfilled, and then feel rather self-gratified—that God must certainly be esteeming them more than those who didn't.

---

17. Ibid.
18. AP: XII.
19. AE 21: 157.

Fasting, then, was a means of drawing attention to oneself, imparting Pharisaic distinctions amongst Christians:

> The end result of all this was that none of this seemed to be of any value unless each one set up his own fast in addition. Now if you put all this fasting together in one pile, it is not worth a heller.[20]

Luther was particularly critical of the four seasonal fasts of the Ember Days. Although they were originally festive in spirit, a celebration of God's providence throughout history, they had taken on a strictly mournful quality by Luther's time.[21] Overall, the laity were less accustomed to hearing about a joyful God than they were about a terrifying one. Accordingly, Luther argued (more from reason and less from exegesis and hermeneutics) that God had abolished mournful fasts and that there were to be only cheerful feasts remembering how God honoured past promises,[22] based on the words of Zechariah that fasting should be filled with "joy, gladness and cheerfulness" (Zech 8:19).[23] In short, Luther argued that a time needs to be set aside to remember how God has fulfilled our needs and answered our prayers, yet this would be most appropriately done in a feast not a fast. Furthermore, because these observances were forced upon the Christians, Luther's words appear to be reacting against the clergy of his day who did not make reflection upon their customs and their contingent meanings a priority. On the contrary, the customs became ridiculous, arbitrary rules existing for their own sake. The violation of one of these ecclesiastical rules resulted in severe spiritual punishment. For instance, in *A Discussion on How Confession Should Be Made* we are informed that,

> if someone has unexpectedly swallowed a few drops of liquid, or has taken a bit of medicine, they keep him away from the sacrament completely and declare it a sin, even the greatest of sins. I wonder where such people get the authority to establish these laws and confuse the consciences with sins they themselves invented... The common people are persuaded that it is heretical to eat butter or eggs on fast days. So atrociously do the laws of men rage in the church of God![24]

20. AE 21:157.
21. *New Catholic Encyclopedia*, 296.
22. AE 20: 75.
23. AE 20:86
24. AE 39: 39-40.

Even if Luther is exaggerating here, his point is that an overemphasis on externalities leads to legalism. Focusing on the works of man inevitably erodes the foundation of Faith—or "conscience"—which is grounded in Jesus the Christ. Not only are these 'man-declared sins' "atrocious", but they are treated as *worse* than the 'God-declared sins':

> We freely delighted in the people's superstition, indeed, in our tyranny, without in any way caring that God's commandments are considered a joke everywhere, as long as people fear and turn pale at *our* laws. No-one calls an adulterer a heretic; fornication is a light sin; even schisms and discords, inspired, preserved, and increased by the authority and in the name of the church, are merits; but to eat meat on Friday is the greatest of all heresies. This is what we teach and permit to be taught to the people of God.[25](italics mine)

Sadly, these pitfalls are with us still today. We encounter the same monastic errors in fasters today. Most contemporary literature is written by so-called "evangelicals" who repeatedly strive to prescribe fasts according to the types and circumstances of those presented in the Old Testament. By assessing the kind and duration of Biblical fasts, present-day Christians are challenged to, for lack of a better word, 'match-up' their fasts with those of the Old Testament and practice them in corresponding fashion, thereby receiving the same benefits and results as the Old Testament saints.[26] These authors regard it as crucial that the *way* we fast be identical to that exhibited in the Old Testament. By documenting what was fasted, for how long, and in precisely what way, the reader is given all the information necessary to carry out 'spiritually effective' fasts. Such approaches not only reflect a

---

25. Ibid.

26. For instance, *Fasting for Spiritual Breakthrough*, by Elmer L. Towns, one of the most elaborate expositions of this system that I myself have discovered, presents fasting as something that *we* must do in order to experience true spiritual freedom, insinuating that what Christ has already done is not enough. This semi-Pelagian system tells the faster not only why and for what to fast, but also from what foods to fast and for how long according to the Biblical examples: part of the day (Dan 6:18); one day (Lev 23:27); three days (Matt 15:32; Mk 8:2-3; Acts 9:9); seven days (1 Sam 31:11-13; I Chron 10:11-12; 2 Sam 12:15-18,21-23); fourteen days (Acts 27:33); three weeks (Dan 10:2,3); forty days (Exodus 34:28; 1 Kings 19:8; Mt 4:1,2; Lk 4:1-2), etc. Proper distinctions between normal fasts (only liquids), absolute fasts (short and no water), and partial fasts (certain foods; limited eating; rotation fasts) and distinctions amongst foods (fasting from grapes and grape products; only partaking in vegetarian dishes as in Dan 1:12-16) are considered crucial in effecting the desired outcome.

bizarre hermeneutical principle and turn devotion into a science, but worse yet, they imply that God is either unholy and impressed with our good works or that He is impersonal and machine-like with buttons which, when pushed correctly, will cause Him to operate in a predictable manner. "In losing sight of the [true] purpose of fasting, one can easily fall prey to self-admiration, vanity, self importance and impatient arrogance".[27]

Encouraging such ascetic formulas is rebuked by God today in the same way that it was in Isaiah 58 when such abuses actually impeded the recovery of post-exilic Israel.[28] In the eyes of the Israelites who believed themselves to be on good terms with God, fasting was supposed to be of some worth and merit. Yet, to paraphrase, the Lord says, "Is *this* what you call a fast? Is *this* supposed to impress your holy and glorious God? You fast for one day, one month, one lifetime, *big deal!*" No external piety but only true righteousness (received from the coming Messiah) pleases God and could change their situation.[29] Like these Israelites who saw their fasting as a formulaic way of "getting something out of God" instead of an activity flowing out of a repentant and burdened heart, trusting in their own pious ascetic works instead of in God,[30] and then questioning whether or not God was living up to His part of the covenant when their fasting "didn't work",[31] these modern-day fasters often lead their followers into the same damnable errors and dilemmas.

The proper Lutheran response to this legalism is to recognize firstly that fasting doesn't reveal to us how well we do it, but like all the commands of God, rather reveals how poorly. *Lex semper accusat*: the "Law always accuses" and, thus, chases us to Christ Jesus who has perfectly fulfilled the law and destroyed its condemning power over us at His cross. Secondly, for the repentant sinner who does not seek to grow closer to God by his own efforts but instead trusts in the works of our precious Saviour, fasting is then cherished as an activity that does not belong to the sphere of Law, but rather to that of Christian liberty. Fasting is a fruit of faith, an expression of the sanctified life which happens by no other means than by returning to Christ and His forgiveness; daily, hourly, and with every breath that we breathe. Fasting and repentance go hand in hand. It can be done with

27. Loughlin, *Thomas Aquinas and the importance of fasting to the Christian life*, 359.
28. Leupold, *Exposition of Isaiah II*, 283.
29. Ibid., 283. See Appendix I.
30. Young, *The Book of Isaiah*, 417.
31. Buttrick, *The Book of Isaiah*, 679.

profound joy because of the place to which it leads us: the home of our loving Lord, and the sacramental feast of his forgiveness. We will explore this dimension of fasting in more depth in a later chapter. For now, it cannot be overemphasized that fasting should be, according to Luther's *Avoiding the Doctrine of Men*, "free and voluntary in both day and food."[32]

> Christ didn't institute fasting by means of laws, but he said, "when the bridegroom is taken from them, then they will fast in that day (Mark 2:20). Go sell all that you possess (Matt 19:21). Then fasting will follow readily.[33]

As a matter of fact, Luther presumes that Christians will fast! Yet when they do so for the wrong reason, as an attempt to fulfill a Law in an effort to merit God's favour, their fasting is useless and even harmful. During the Middle Ages, because fasting had become a means of atoning for sins as part of a system of efforts at increasing in degrees of holiness, it naturally became a means of strengthening the virtues of which this holiness consisted. For instance, the virtue of temperance took on a new importance in personal practices of piety. For many still today

> temperance is conceived as that by which one brings moderation to eating, drinking, and the pleasures of bed. It is a medicine, so to speak, to be taken when excesses in these areas erupt . . . Temperance, then, is a bitter remedy, an austerity imposed upon oneself, depriving one of the common bodily pleasures and is no more than a quantitative affair determined by the severity of the problem. It is little wonder, then, that many understand and even experience temperance as a misery . . . a frustration that one must bear, a law to be fulfilled in an effort to appease a God who is, at the end of the day, a "kill joy".[34]

Luther did not oppose virtuous living. He rather rejected all legalism and burdensome attitudes towards Godly virtues. Instead, he shifted decision making on such matters of personal piety away from the arena of ecclesiastical rules and towards the arena of Christian freedom: only the individual can rightfully determine fasting's proper usage since it needs to be evaluated by personal motivation which may differ between people. Fasting looks different from person to person. Because we all have our own unique set of

---

32. AE 35: 134.
33. AE 24: 356.
34. Loughlin, *Thomas Aquinas and the importance of fasting to the Christian life*, 343.

idols hidden within our hearts from which we seek deliverance, people will never fast in the exact same way. We fast from that which is most difficult for us to 'give up'. Seafood lovers who eat at Red Lobster on Fridays and pig-out on deep-fried calamari, or vegetarians who wouldn't be tempted to eat meat in any case, can hardly be considered fasting. Christians abstaining from what they already abstain from isn't much of a fast. As the old joke goes: "What are you giving up for lent this year?" "I figured that I would do the same as last year since it worked so well then." "What was that?" "Fasting." Fasting from fasting is hardly a fast.

When the Biblical heroes fast, they fast from what they love too much, such as Daniel who chooses to forego tasty food, or wine or meat (Dan 10:2-3). Accordingly, Luther teaches that

> Everyone has to take a look at himself and judge his own feelings. We are not all alike, and so no one can set up a general rule. Everyone must impose or adjust the fasting in relation to his own strength and to his feelings about how much his own flesh requires ... *It should be left up to the discretion of every individual.*[35] (italics mine)

In fact, it *must* be left up to the individual, in order for it to have the desired effect. After all, we ought to fast from those things which we desire the most. And desires vary. Food is a necessity of life, and for the ancients it was very precious since it was often scarce and not distributed in egalitarian ways. We in North America are severely spoiled. We take for granted our rich surplus of food and all the diversity thereof. Abstaining from food helps to confront such arrogance. Yet abstaining from other things that are important to us reveals our truest gods; fasting, say, from the television or the internet for a month, or from listening to music, or from going to the pub, or from golfing, etc. Fasting reveals to us those things that really matter: our idols, which are nothing other than those things in which we trust or cannot live without, so that we can be rid of them, replacing them with Christ. Our sight is clouded by the mammon and desires of this world. Fasting helps to free us from idolatry by taking all those things upon which we depend and giving them up for a while so that they can be restored to good use by our being made aware that all we really need in life is God. Only He satisfies. As a community of believers, we *know* this to be true. But *believing* it is an *individual* affair.

---

35. AE 21: 162.

Because of the personal nature of fasting as it pertains to particular passions of the flesh, the Eastern Abbott, St. Symeon the New Theologian (942-1022), speaks about fasting as healing souls by addressing the idiosyncratic illnesses of each one. In one it quiets the fevers and impulses of the flesh; in another, it assuages bad temper; in another, it stirs up zeal; in another, it controls unbridled tongue, etc.[36] When fasting is driven by faith, it produces different fruits in different Christians, yet all of them are good eating.

In general, Christians keep to the "middle of the road" concerning the practice of any pious activity, always eating and drinking in moderation.[37] Luther asserts that it is indeed good to fast, to "become bridled to follow the Holy Spirit", but not to let oneself "become unhealthy from neglect of bodily needs, like the great St. Bernard" before Bernard came to his senses.[38] Likewise, in the *Catholic Epistles*, Luther rejects those who declare Christian freedom in destructive antinomian fashion and choose not to fast.[39]

Luther spoke on the subject with obvious passion and conviction, precisely because he himself had experienced these abominable traditions first hand. Luther was not unfamiliar with the effects of these legalistic fasts: he himself was one of those whose conscience had been burdened. In the *Smalcald Articles* he confesses how he used to practice all the ceremonies as a monk to fight against evil thoughts, and in attempts to be holy, believed that perfection in human works was actually achievable.[40] He himself was one of the hypocrites that he so passionately condemns! Fortunately, the Lord revealed to him his sin and the diabolical essence of the fasting in which he partook. And so out of thanksgiving Luther warns us today of how easily fasting can turn into masochism and sadomasochism, a demented means of inverting the design of God upon our bodies. In contrast to the beliefs of some Gnostic groups and modern philosophies, our Creator wants us to honour and protect the flesh with which he has entrusted us.

> The unnatural fasts of gloomy hypocrites do not care for the flesh God has given them but are so exhausted by tormenting themselves that they become altogether useless.[41]

36. Symeon, *The Discourses*, 168.
37. AE 28: 15, 14.
38. AE 30: 27.
39. Ibid., 28
40. SA: Part III, III.
41. AE 4: 14-15.

St. Jerome was one of those who suffered from such self-abuse. In his *Letters*, he writes that when he was young and his flesh rebelled, he subdued it by weeks of fasting with little success:

> my face was pale from fasting, but my mind burned with passionate desires; within my freezing body the fires of sex seethed, even though the flesh had already died in me as a man.[42]

Even though we Christians are to devalue our bodies relationally (in terms of our relationship with the Triune God) and even despise our sinful bodies, we are to value our baptized bodies, intrinsically purchased and redeemed by the Blood of Christ and His atoning death and sacrifice. It is this practice which distinguishes us from Stoics, Gnostics, and Christians of all stripes that devalue the material world as an inappropriate means of the communication of God's divine gifts and grace. In his *Lectures on Genesis*, the Reformer asserts that,

> The body has been given to us by God, not that we should kill it with fasting or vigils, but that we should care for it with food, drink, clothing, sleep, and medicine. In Col 2:23 Paul censures the hypocrites who do not spare their bodies.[43]

Luther confesses that he did not always believe this Gospel message:

> In the monastery I, too, was once such a murderer and the worst persecutor of my own body; for I used to fast, pray, watch, and fatigue myself beyond my strength. This means inviting and bringing death upon oneself.[44]

Most of Luther's clerical contemporaries however, were not as pious as he. Luther's writings are a reaction against the hypocrisy and contradictions found in those fasts as well. In 1526 he exhorts: "The monks fast but other sins run rampant."[45] For instance, "the Romanists dishonour God by making a mockery of their own proclaimed fasts as they often competed with each other in fasting."[46] What Julianus Pomerius, from whom we have some of the earliest writings of pastoral instruction in the West, already observed in the fifth century, that the monks of his day fasted with an unchristian

---

42. Jerome, *Letters*, 69.
43. AE 17: 113.
44. Ibid., 113.
45. AE 20: 142.
46. Jerome, *Letters*, 170.

spirit while "craving human applause",[47] held true in Luther's day. These observations caused St. Jerome to teach that it is better to eat in moderation and be thankful rather than piously fasting with anger in the heart.[48] He advocates that fasting "a little bit each day" is better than ending the fast with "gorging" as was often the case.[49] This was routinely witnessed by Luther and recorded in his *Table Talks*: "to every day of fasting belonged three days of gorging".[50] Furthermore many of the Papist man-made rules concerning particular fasts were so simple and arbitrary that they were offensive to God, insofar as they belittled His holiness and made His wrath appear easily appeased. They were just too easy! Abstaining from meat on Friday while feasting on luxurious seafood is hardly a sacrifice!

The abuses that Luther reacted against stretch back to the Old Testament era. The Bible documents numerous incidents in which fasting is practiced for the wrong reasons and in the wrong spirit. In 1 Kings 21:9-13, we learn how fasting was sometimes practiced to cover up other sinful motives and distract from sinful practices, illustrated by Queen Jezebel when she had Naboth unjustly killed after calling a fast. The insincere, half-hearted fast is also the kind rejected by God in Jeremiah 14:11-12 and the kind God detests in Saul's foolish ordering of a fast as a malicious means of avenging his enemies as in 1 Samuel 14:24. The best exposition of this hypocrisy is seen in Isaiah 58 which condemns insincere fasts and insincere worship in general, which try to manipulate God, minimize His holiness and basically separate the formal practice from internal devotion to God [see Appendix I]. Although humbly afflicting oneself in order to attract divine pity (by indicating to God our sincerity and trust in His holy will) may arouse divine mercy in Joshua 7:6, the people's fasting is rejected since it is conducted with mixed motives: the mourning rites which were observed by Joshua did not constitute penitence but rather protests designed to induce mercy.[51]

This same hypocrisy and abuse of fasting continued into the New Testament era. Fasting for ascetic reasons was demanded by a false teacher in the early Church, who confused Law and Gospel and limited the full appreciation of all of God's gifts, including food (1 Tim 4:3-5). Most important

---

47. Pomerius, *Ancient Christian Writers*, 128.
48. Jerome, *Letters*, 173.
49. Ibid., 148.
50. AE 54:178.
51. Lambert, *Fasting as a Penitential Rite*, 496.

however, were the words of our Lord in regard to the subject. Jesus strongly criticized the Pharisees, many of whom fasted for appearances rather than as genuine worship (Matt 6:16-18).

We discover from our Lord Jesus' own words the importance of proper motivation in fasting. Even in the Gospel according to St. Matthew 6:16-18, Christ was not so much concerned about whether a faster could keep his fasting hidden from others, but whether the fast was practiced for the right reasons: the Pharisees fasted for outward show and public recognition (i.e. instead of seeking rewards from man in public, receiving rewards from God in secret[52]). The Pharisees (here referred to as 'hypocrites') normally fasted only in the daytime for all to see, and by their appearance [since much stress was laid by Jewish 'pietists' on gestures in fasting[53]] all men knew of their fasting. Fasting was a pinnacle sign of religious piety [seen in Luke 18:12 (the Pharisee was unquestionably more religiously pious than the tax-gatherer!)] and this is evidently why John the Baptizer was held in such high regard. Fasting was characteristic of his and his disciples' somewhat monastic lifestyle (Mark 2:18). They were at one with the 'exemplary righteous' of Judaism[54] and most lay people were impressed by their superior piety and devotion. Yet God desires a sincere fast, and one offered to Him alone. This can only happen when eyes are focused solely upon God, which is most easily achieved in a private setting.

Luther too was opposed to fasts for outward show. In the spirit of what Christ said, he comments on the Pharisaical perversion of fasting which was neither a means of controlling or disciplining their own bodies or praising and thanking God, but a device for being seen and admired.[55] Although lengthy, this comment regarding Christ's Sermon on the Mount is worth citing in its entirety:

---

52. At the same time, a Christian must remain wary of the language of rewards which can be misunderstood to undermine God's grace and righteousness in Christ alone. Fasting is not meritorious, but rather has an effect on a generous deity who is all too eager to shower gifts upon his beloved children (Lambert, *Fasting as a Penitential Rite*, 511). When my children behave well and in ways that bring me joy, I am naturally inclined to give them treats and privileges. When they misbehave, I may deprive them of these temporal blessings, but their status as my dear precious children remains unchanged. It is one thing to hold that our generous God rewards His children. It is quite another thing to go seeking rewards from our generous God.

53. Kittel, *The Theological Dictionary of the New Testament*, 930.

54. Ibid.

55. AE 21: 155.

> The origin of fasting among the Jews was in the prescription of Moses (Lev 23:27), that they should fast for approximately fourteen days in a row during the Feast of Atonement in the autumn... In addition the Pharisees had their own special fast, by which they did something more and acquired a holier reputation than the others... whatever is common to all cannot become the special boast of one. This is why they had to undertake many special fasts [and boasted even before Christ: Mt 9:14]... in addition they made use of distinctive gestures and marks to let it be known when they were fasting.
>
> Now Christ comes along and teaches the opposite when he says, 'If you want to fast, then fast in such a way that you do not wear a sad expression. Wash and anoint your face so that you seem to be merry, happy, and cheerful, like a person on a holiday. That way no one will be able to tell the difference between your fasting and festivities'. It was the custom of the Jews to sprinkle themselves with perfumes and to anoint their heads so that their whole body was fragrant when they were having a celebration or wanted to be cheerful. If you fast in this way, so that it is a matter between you and your Father alone, then you have fasted rightly, and it is pleasing to Him. This does not make it wrong to wear poor clothes on a fast day or to go without washing, but it *rejects the motivation* when you do this for the sake of acquiring a reputation, and when you use special gestures to make people stare.[56]

Luther addresses here the *motivation* for fasting. The *spirit* of the fasting, or of any Christian devotional activity, is what counts. "Almsgiving, praying and fasting are all to be done in secret; what the Father sees in secret He rewards openly."[57] Fasting ought to really then be seen as a fruit of this spirit, or *the* Spirit (i.e. the Holy Spirit). A *sincere faith* will produce *sincere fruits*, like fasting. In the *Apology of the Augsburg Confession* Melanchthon insists that fasting is a natural pious expression of the Christian Faith: "We believe that God's glory and command require penitence to produce good fruits, and that good fruits like true fasting, prayer, and charity have his command."[58] Luther sums up the idea nicely in his comments on Malachi 3:14:

> "it is vain to serve God. What is the good of our walking as in mourning, etc." To sum up, the Lord is saying here that fasting is

---

56. AE 21: 156.
57. Ibid.,163.
58. AP: XII.

not done for Him, that all these things are worthless because he has not commanded them, but that he approves of those things which stem from a good source: from a faithful heart. You see, once the heart is sanctified and pure, whatever comes afterwards is also pure and holy, whether one fasts or eats, whether one keeps watch or falls asleep.[59]

In appreciation of the Christian spirit of fasting, we must assert along with Julianus Pomerius that those who do not fast but thank God for His gifts surpass in humility those who fast without gratitude,[60] since fasting is meant to both deepen our faith and increase our love. For, as Jerome shares, "we punish our bodies with vigils, fasts and labors; but we neglect love, which is the Lord and master of all works."[61] The sacramental character of fasting is so tightly intertwined with a sincere observance that the absence of the former results from the neglect of the latter. Yet not just any sincere motivation will do. One can be sincere in one's hopes that one's fasts will merit God's favour and be wrong. Love, as the fruit of faith in Christ's righteousness, ought always to be both the cause and the effect of wholesome practices like fasting. Only then do they "[strengthen] virtue"[62] and lead us along a road of ascetic living . . . whether we like it or not.

59. AE 20: 78.
60. Pomerius, *Ancient Christian Writers*, 99.
61. AE 27: 55.
62. Pomerius, *Ancient Christian Writers*, 126.

2

FRIEND OF THE ASCETIC

HAVING TALKED ABOUT WHAT fasting is not, let us now turn our discussion towards what fasting is. Because of his personal experiences within the medieval church, Luther was naturally less comfortable than successors like Martin Chemnitz—the "second Martin" of the Reformation—in celebrating the gift of fasting:

> On account of the papalist abuses some are so afraid of the teaching about fasting that they shrink back when they only hear the term "fasting" mentioned, as though they had heard either murder or adultery; and some reject the whole teaching about fasting without discrimination among human traditions.[1]

The central idea of fasting is the voluntary denial of an otherwise normal function for the sake of more disciplined spiritual living. In short, fasting disciplines the body for the sake of a higher goal. The Egyptian mystics of the fourth century who devoted their lives to solitude, the Desert Fathers, spoke about the body as if it were a wild animal that needed taming in order to be of any use to the owner. They believed that this discipline was best achieved in the wilderness, the place where the Lord Jesus Himself wrestled with the temptations of the devil. The idea was that, if one could beat the devil in his home turf, so to speak, one could have victory over him everywhere else. Although these mystics may have overemphasized

---

1. Chemnitz, *Martin. Examination of the Council of Trent IV*, 255.

the human potential in overcoming sin—instead of relying entirely upon Christ—we have still inherited a wealth of treasures from these Christian brothers (and sisters) to assist us in our earthly pilgrimage and spiritual battle; lessons gravitating around the harm done to our spiritual lives by an idolatrous treatment of our bodies and its "needs". They repeatedly pointed out how "the Spirit must brand the flesh that it may live".[2] Human passions entangle the life of the soul and therefore must be controlled. It is by *ascesis*, or training, that the body is disciplined, like an athlete. St. Paul likened spiritual discipline to the physical discipline of present-day athletes who punish their bodies, pummelling and subduing them, for the sake of winning the prize (1 Cor 9:25-27).[3] Fasting then is cooperating with God in the sanctified life, in helping set the conditions (or, at the very least, not hindering them) for this holy work. As Christians we can either choose to work with God, willingly resting in the hands of the great Sculptor as he molds us in His likeness, or we can choose to resist His Spirit, working against God's refining process in our lives. Martin Chemnitz explains it like this:

> If fasting is practiced and ordered to this end, that the flesh may be coerced, subjugated, and reduced to servitude, lest it contend against the spirit and hinder and disturb its actions either by its willfulness or its indifference, but that we may have a body obedient and fit for spiritual things and for the performance of its duties, lest satiety and sloth goad us into sinning but that the mind may be admonished and become more fit for spiritual desires, so that the spirit may be able the more ardently and willingly to give and devote itself to repentance, prayer, and other exercises of piety, as we shall presently show by examples—if, I say, fasting is practiced to this end, then finally it is pleasing to God. Therefore, Jerome says rightly that fasting is not a virtue, but a step toward virtue.[4]

Fasting tills the soil of the heart for the seeds of virtue to take root. It surrenders our will and power to God and allows Him to fashion us in an inimitable way. The sanctified life is not easy. It can be painful. It compels Christians to behold that which is hard to behold, and to embrace that which is hard to embrace.[5] But it is all good. Fasting becomes an

2. Waddell, *The Desert Fathers*, 10.
3. Pelikan, *The Illustrated Jesus*, 150.
4. Chemnitz, *Examination of the Council of Trent IV*, 264.
5. *Thomas Aquinas and the importance of fasting to the Christian life*. Stephen Loughlin, 356.

opportunity to bring all that one is, consciously and deliberately, into the contemplation of and submission to the things of God.[6] Deliberate efforts to self-inflict suffering and stage an environment of impoverishment are common training tactics for soldiers in the military. The idea is to recreate scenarios in a controlled environment in order to allow the soldier to be better equipped when experiencing the real thing. In crisis situations, there is often little time to think and decide how to react. Instead, "muscle memory" refers to an automatic default to survival reactions learned and repeated in training environments. Training within specialized military forces includes days of containment as a hostage by trained actors who are authorized to inflict a certain degree of violence upon their "detainees". The experience is intended to mimic the horrors of a real-life situation so that, if ever subjected to the real thing, the soldier will revert to their training and act accordingly. Perfection is not the goal. War is messy. Christians are spiritual soldiers and there are never shortcuts to good training. Fasting isn't about perfecting ourselves in holy living and self-righteousness. It is about taming the Old Adam, and trapping him under the waters of Holy Baptism, so that he is somewhat manageable until he is finally annihilated in Christian death. Fasting involves surviving a spiritual war with self and the human experience of suffering, until the trumpet of victory is sounded when our Lord returns. Voluntarily depriving oneself of pleasures in an effort to self-mortify prepares us for the seasons of life when fasting is involuntary; when illness, persecution, famine and poverty (both physical and spiritual) strike. The feelings, sentiments and struggles that we face on our deathbeds will not seem as unfamiliar or terrifying, having had a taste of some of them by our deliberate exercises in spiritual discipline and ascesis. For the Israelites, there was "a fine line between the undesired dissolution of the body wrought by illness and the purposeful dissolution of the body wrought by fasting".[7]

Unlike the Gnostics who drove a wedge between the things of the body and the things of the soul, the Church Fathers (with Biblical precedent) rightly presumed an intricate connection between the body and soul. The mastering of the one helps bring peace to the other. Disciplining our

---

6. Ibid.
7. Lambert, *Fasting as a Penitential Rite*, 489.

earthly desires by fasting can help lead to victory in our spiritual struggles;[8] controlling these desires occasions invulnerability in other spheres.[9]

Fasting strengthens our spirit by controlling the flesh. One Rabbi comments, "When we control our appetites on [fast days], we remember that on other days, too, we can be masters, not slaves, of our desires."[10] While training nuns, an Iberian Father, Leander of Seville (540-600) says this: "Hard flesh must be subject to fasts and so thoroughly held in check that it will be subject to the law of the mind and the commands of the soul like a maidservant."[11] Likewise Luther, while commenting on St. Paul's words in 1 Cor 9:27, "I pommel my body and subdue it", says:

> if we do not restrain the flesh [by fasting], we are overcome with satiety and become complacent and idle with the result that we indulge and pamper the desires of our flesh. Therefore we must be diligent at all times because God commands it.[12]

God commands fasting for *our* sake since by becoming comfortable with our sins (especially specific sins of which we are aware like habitual sinful behaviors or attitudes) we end up victimizing and enslaving ourselves.[13] Contrariwise, when the physical appetite is controlled, we develop some

---

8. Waddell, *The Desert Fathers*, 88.

9. Ibid., 62. The Hebrews who obviously shared a similar ethos with the Christians believed that fasting like other spiritual activities (e.g. prayer, repentance, worship, etc.) were "full body" experiences, activities involving the *entire* self (Westerman, *Isaiah 40-66*, 336). In contradistinction to present-day Gnostic beliefs, the mind and body were logically distinct yet temporally inseparable. For instance, the actual translation for "soul" is "the self" demonstrating that dividing the person, who is a breathing living creature together in both body and soul, is, for all practical purposes, impossible. The Hebrew conceived of the person as consisting of an inner self (*nephesh*) and an outer appearance (*shem*): what one is to self and what one appears to others who observe him, namely his reputation or name (Zodiates, *The Hebrew-Greek Key Study Bible*, 1637). This is why in Col 2:18, the phrase "humiliation of mind" echoes the Semitic periphrasis "affliction of one's soul" (Freedman, *Isaiah II*, 773). The language of 'humbling the body' can correctly be applied to both mind and body since both make up the soul. The discussion also sheds light on Christ's rebuke of the Pharisees' fasting, which was less about afflicting the soul (i.e. a "whole person" experience) and more about building up an outward appearance, a pious name and reputation for themselves.

10. Knobel, *Jewish Fasts: Gates of the Seasons*, 50.

11. Iberian Fathers, *Sayings of the Egyptian Fathers*, 212.

12. AP: XV.

13. Towns, *Fasting for Spiritual Breakthrough*, 29.

stamina to control the emotional appetite. Luther teaches us from St. Paul's First Letter to Timothy that,

> we should live purely, fast and keep watch that we do not give our passions an opportunity to dominate our spirits through an unrestrained life. Fasting helps us to control these passions.[14]

Fasting and piety are, in fact,

> necessary bodily training which lead to the controlling of the passions, though one should not trust in them [and] recognize that they are not as great as Godliness and Christian service.[15]

In a culture obsessed with good eating, where discussion of food dominates much of our social intercourse (e.g. consider the popularity of "all-you-can-eat" buffets as a favourite form of entertainment), Christians must guard against this culturally specific idol. In this sense, fasting liberates us from these imprisoning cultural idols.

> A fast offers freedom from the usual routine: our food choices, our most basic necessities, are no longer determined by the often unreflected criteria of our everyday lives ... man liberating himself from a life chained solely to necessity and unbreakable law.[16]

On his discussion of Romans 13:13, Luther quotes John Cassian (360-435), who introduced Eastern monasticism to the West, saying,

> fasting is one of the strongest weapons of a Christian, [since] gluttony is one of the most potent machines of the devil, and gluttony is often the most difficult vice to overcome.[17]

Although erring in some respects, St. John of the Cross speaks some wise words concerning the benefits of fasting:

> When one loves something together with God he undoubtedly makes little of God. We have a figure of this in the Exodus where we read that God did not give the children of Israel the heavenly manna until they exhausted the flour brought from Egypt (Ex 16:3-4, 15). The meaning here is that first a total renunciation is needed, for this bread of angels is disagreeable to the palate of anyone desirous of tasting human food. Persons feeding on other

---

14. AE 28: 355.
15. Ibid., 321.
16. Vassa Larin, *Feasting and Fasting According to the Byzantine Typikon*, 142.
17. AE 25: 482.

strange tastes not only become incapable of the divine Spirit, but even greatly anger His divine Majesty because in their aspirations for spiritual food they are not satisfied with God alone, but intermingle with their aspiration a desire and affection for other things.[18]

Yet fasting is not so much about controlling *one* bodily appetite, as about *all* the appetites of the flesh. The ancients did not condemn the quality of foods as much as they did the concupiscence for them and strove to avoid the food or drink which they personally *craved*.[19] St. Paul included idolatries and *luxuries* in his list of the works of the flesh.[20] Our fasts offer to God all the things that we value the most. St. Paul advises young couples to abstain from sex for a short period of time, and to pray together instead (1 Cor 7:5)! Luther agrees that a couple's choice to freely chasten themselves for a period of one week or two[21] is an effective way of presenting to God those things which consume far too much of our thoughts and time. Thomas Aquinas saw "abstinence as the virtue that governs one's enjoyment of the basic sensual pleasures, particularly those connected with the consumption of food;"[22] a way of keeping our priorities "in check" and preventing them from becoming an idol in our lives. Fasting allows us to bring some of the many false gods in which we trust to our one true God in whom we lack trust. In fasting, God exposes all of these idols so that they can be smashed into pieces. Yet food and drink can easily become the primary created things which we believe we cannot live without, and around which our lives revolve. This holds especially true in countries and cultures where hunger is rampant and there is a lack of food. Being of European descent, when I was growing up, skipping a meal was unacceptable because my parents were raised in an environment in which there was often not enough food to go around the table, a foreign notion to my affluent generation. We treat our grumbling stomachs as a national crisis that deserves immediate response. We wonder if going to bed hungry may mean that we don't wake up at all! However, fasters can testify how little food and drink we actually need to live, and how a simple diet can provide all that we need. Treasuring

18. John of Cross, *Selected Writings*, 70-71.
19. Jerome, *Letters*, 94.
20. Augustine, *Ancient Christian Writers*, 168.
21. AE 28: 14-15.
22. Loughlin, *Thomas Aquinas and the importance of fasting to the Christian life*, 344.

the first commandment, trusting only in Christ and not in other things, involves putting these created things in their proper place so that they do not distract us from the Creator. In this sense, we strive to fast *from all things* at *all times*.

> True fasting involves more than merely abstaining from food in the evening, which is only the smallest part of it. True fasting consists in the disciplining and restraining of your body, which pertains not only to eating, drinking, and sleeping but also to your leisure, your pleasure/friends, and to everything that may delight your body or that you do to provide for it and take care of it . . . a means of curbing and humbling the flesh. Afflict the soul and body . . . the ancient fathers withheld everything from their bodies, to the limit of natural endurance . . . humble your body and withhold from it whatever pleases and gratifies it.[23]

In brief, fasting is abstaining from all of our carnal desires. With St. Jerome, we ought to strive not to be eager to eat, but to restrain ourselves; desiring to satisfy our hunger only, yet "neither with gourmet rich foods nor with gluttony of common foods."[24] Moreover, fasting includes the control of *all* passions. As alluded to in Joel 2:15, fasting is not merely abstaining from food but from all pleasures and delights[25] as a way of setting boundaries for ourselves.[26]

> Everyone is commanded to live a moderate, sober and disciplined life, not for one day or one year, but for every day and always.[27]

Generally, then, fasting involves a willingness to submit to self-discipline. "How can we atone for our excesses towards others unless we can curb appetites which depend on no one but ourselves?"[28] Although this use of the word "atone" is rather unpalatable for the Christian—perhaps "deal with" or "reconcile" may have been a better choice—the point is stated well: this visible submission to discipline is truly a way of denying ourselves and taking up the cross (Mark 8:34).[29] In a way, John the Baptizer's wish that "I

---

23. AE 21: 160.
24. Jerome, *Letters*, 95.
25. AE 18: 100.
26. Knobel, *Jewish Fasts: Gates of the Seasons*,146.
27. AE 21: 162.
28. Knobel, *Jewish Fasts: Gates of the Seasons*,146.
29. Wimmer, *Fasting in the New Testament*,120.

must decrease" so that Christ may increase (John 3:30) is continued and manifested in the humility of fasting.

Fasting aims to compel the body to serve the spirit and not the other way around. Otherwise, our passions control us and abuse us, leading us into sin and vice. Specific foods are not condemned, but carnal desires are. "Abstinence means controlling these desires [since] God says he is a God of order and not chaos"[30] and so,

> You may eat either fish or meat, but no more than your real need requires, to keep your body from being injured or incapacitated and yet to hold it in check and to keep it busy so that it does not become idle or lazy or lewd . . . .[31]

The dynamics of this process are quite simple. Abstinence makes our minds alert and renders our bodies agile. In a sense, our spirit overcompensates for our weak bodies, and beats them into submission. This is not to be confused with stoic ideas which have a humanistic understanding of 'spirit', normally equating it with the mind. In his discussion on Holy Baptism, Luther asserts that it is in essence God's Spirit dwelling in us which tames the flesh.[32] Furthermore, to control a passion is not to rid oneself of it. There is a time for feasting and a time for passionate expression. Zeal for the Word of God and cravings to do good deeds are noble passions. Yet the passions of the flesh often crowd out these holier passions of the spirit.

> Our mind is hampered and called back from the contemplation of God, because we are led into captivity by the passions of the flesh.[33]

We are freer and at greater peace when we have controlled, not deleted, our human passions. Although we will never achieve complete freedom until our resurrections, God welcomes and expects our attempts to obey His Law as an expression of faith, when we strive for a disciplined life in our walk in the grace of Christ. Fasting, then, is an expression of praise. In fact, the entire Christian life can be viewed as one continuous fast, the logistics being left to individual conviction. In reference to Anna the prophetess, Luther reminds us in one of his Epiphany sermons that fasting strives,

---

30. Pomerius, *Ancient Christian writers*, 96.
31. AE 21: 161.
32. AE 35:37.
33. Waddell, *The Desert Fathers*, 10.

> to quell the sin and the flesh which [God] wants quelled ... Anna who *served God day and night with fasting and prayer*, the prophetess, she did not have special fast days, or make distinctions between foods ... St. Paul teaches in 2 Corinthians 6:5, stating that in fasting we should show ourselves as servants of God. Chastising the body and sin is serving God. Anna's *whole life was one of fasting. She did not literally fast day and night with no interruption.*[34] *(italics mine)*

When Christians fast we, too, are characterized in this way: as fasters. A soldier is not a soldier for one battle or for a day. It is his identity, in both times of war and peace. We, too, are soldiers. Appreciating the power of fasting exemplified in the lives of many saints, it is no wonder that the pre-Enlightenment Church almost unanimously spoke about fasting as a means of "spiritual warfare" against the devil. By subduing the flesh, the instrument by which the devil often tempts his enemies, the Spirit of the *Christus Victor* is victorious.[35] In the Old Testament, fasting was a common ritual for preparing for holy war (1 Sam 14:24)[36]—a "necessary evil" in ensuring the birth of the Saviour of all nations—and Israel prepared herself by weeping and fasting before her battle against the mighty Benjamin (Judges 20:26). These historic incidents act as metaphors for the Christian's preparation for war against the demonic world. According to Jewish thought, fasting "drives out [evil] spirits."[37] The *language* of Christendom mirrors this historic motif. St. Maximus (580-662), devotional writer and one of the main architects of Byzantine theology, states:

> For our fasts are camps for us, which protect us from the diabolical onslaught. And they are called posts because, when we stand and stay in them, we can parry the strategy of our enemies. It is clear that fasts are armed camps for Christians, and if a person wanders away from them he is devoured by the wasteland of sins.[38]

---

34. AE 52: 139.

35. Because the body is "the 'vehicle of the soul' as the ancients call it, may it not overwhelm the mind because it has been made coarse and fat by too much fulness and too much delicate treatment" (Chemnitz, *Examination of the Council of Trent IV*, 265).

36. Wimmer, *Fasting in the New Testament*, 8.

37. Kittel, *The Theological Dictionary of the New Testament*, 930.

38. Maximus, *Sermons*, 168.

Fasting is a technique by which the devil's hold on us is weakened. It is likened to a weapon along with prayer and almsgiving.[39] "Like prayer wounds from a greater distance than an arrow, fasting is surer protection than a rampart, mercy saves more easily than pillage."[40] Mercy, fasting and prayer are described as our weapons of spiritual warfare.[41]

Speaking in this traditional militaristic language, St. Augustine comments on this particular purpose in fasting:

> Man must fast when a similar struggle with temptation comes [similar to Christ's temptation in the desert]... so that the body may discharge its military service by its discipline and the soul may gain a victory by its humiliation. Hence in this precedent set by our Lord, the fast was occasioned, not by the immersion in the Jordan, but by the [anticipated] temptation of the devil. This is the reason why we fast before solemnizing the Passion of the Lord and why the relaxation of the fast is ended on the fiftieth day of Easter.[42]

Because Christ was victorious over the devil in His fasting during His temptation, we, too, can be victorious in ours... through His! He continues to fight the devil through our fasts, reclaiming this victory for us again and again. Although it is crucial to remember that Christ's fast was different than ours, that He was the Redeemer, the fulfiller of the Law, the perfect faster who perfects all our imperfect fasts in the sight of our Heavenly Father, it is useful to remember that He was also an example for us, just as Luther calls the fastings of the saints "examples for us."[43] Fasting as preparation for spiritual warfare is not a human invention. Similarly, St. Ambrose (339-397), bishop of Milan, instructs his priests:

> The Lord Jesus wishing to make us strong against the temptations of the Devil, fasted when He was about to struggle with him, so that we might know that we cannot otherwise overcome the enticement of evil... Since they say we ought not to fast, let them show us why Christ fasted if not to make His fast an example for us. Then in the words which He later spoke, He taught us that evil

---

39. Ibid., 206.
40. Ibid., 198.
41. Ibid., 298, 206.
42. Augustine, *Sermons on Liturgical Seasons*, 99-100.
43. AE 4:336.

cannot easily be conquered except by our fasting, saying, "this kind of devil is only cast out by prayer and fasting (Matt 17:21).[44]

Evidently, Jesus Himself teaches us that a relationship between fasting and exorcism exists (Matt 17:21; Mark 9:29). To be sure, while casting out devils one must be entirely convinced that the strength and victory belong exclusively to the Lord Jesus Himself. The disciples may have been suffering with some inflated egos which was the cause of their failure. Soldiers that think too highly of themselves are their own worst enemies. In this sense, fasting is a means of reminding us, not of our internal strength, but of our natural weakness, in order to kill the temptation to believe our own intrinsic skills, strengths or abilities are of any value in exorcising a demon. After all, the Holy Scriptures promise: "My grace is sufficient for you, for my power is made perfect in weakness" (2 Cor 12:9). The weapons of the battle belong to our Lord alone, who may loan them to us, yet without losing control or ownership. One soldier friend of mine compared spiritual warfare with a baby holding a bazooka. The enemy is not intimidated by the baby, but the weapon in his tiny frail hands is enough to make him flee in terror. In Holy Baptism we are made children of God. We are all, in fact, infants. Yet the Word of Christ is our weapon. Sadly, many Christians remain unaware of the powerful tools at their fingertips, or are unfamiliar as to how they all work. Like a novice gunman who can't seem to find the trigger, they can easily be overcome by the enemy. Instruction by a faithful pastor in Church and participation in Bible Study are good places to learn about the origin, meaning and practical use of the full armour of God (Eph 6:10-28). They also provide the opportunity to celebrate the One who has so graciously equipped us with all that is required to fight the good fight of faith (1 Tim 6:11-16). In fact, fasting exposes all of our imaginary weapons that we so treasure in our tool box, the ones that don't exist, that arise from self. We are then ready to be directed to the weapons that have been gifted to us in Holy Baptism. If we were to believe what God says we are, if we had faith to see the armour with which we are clothed and the weapons with which we are already equipped, we would never again flinch at an assault by the evil one, not even in the midst of a legion of demons nor demoniacs.

One teenage Christian said bluntly, "fasting is not about how good we do it, but about how much we suck at it". He had a good point. It is easy to give out of abundance but how much joy do we feel when "giving up" means going without? Being hungry doesn't make you friendlier, or

---

44. Ambrose, *Letters*, 326.

make you want to go the extra mile for a stranger in need. Your face doesn't shine with a healthy glow but rather resembles an ashen pall. How generous we become after a delicious holiday feast, in contrast with those moments when we feel ourselves to be "starving to death". Remember Esau? When deprived of only a few things, we become miserable, selfish, animal-like, and our true self as sinner, the old Adam, is embarrassingly revealed. Thank God that we are simultaneously sinner *and saint* in Christ our righteousness in whom "we live and move and have our being" (Acts 17:28).

I once lived in a home that was regularly attacked by skunks. Relying on my own efforts, devices and wisdom in trying to frighten them away—which included a lot of screaming, waving of arms and shaking of fists—was futile. But after a bit of research on the internet, I found that the solution was simpler than I could ever have imagined: leaving a light on and playing some music in my yard. They never came back! Jesus is the Light of the world, who shines brightly in the darkness independent of our aid. His Word is the music that terrifies all hellish hordes. In the spiritual battle in which all Christians are endlessly engaged, fasting is a means of surrendering all of our futile techniques, while prayer is the means of switching on the light and turning up the volume.

Some exegetes argue that because the reference to fasting in the Holy Gospel according to St. Matthew 17:21 is absent from some of the earliest and most reliable manuscripts (*Codex Sinaiticus*, and *B*), it is difficult to believe that God-fearing scribes would have added this material unless it was already part of early oral tradition.[45] We have references to "fleeing to the Lord" in fasting "where evil spirits flee" already present in the pseudepigrapha (T Sim III: 1-6), in which "fleeing" is tantamount to "fasting".[46] The early Tertullian wrote that fasting possesses great power and "if practiced with right intention, it makes a man a friend of God. The demons are aware of that."[47] One account by the seventh-century Spanish writer Braulio Saragosa (585?-651?) tells of a Senator Honoraius who asked St. Emilian to drive out a demon in Parpalines. St. Emilian declared a fast,

---

45. This Judeo-Christian view was echoed in other religions as well. The Greeks fasted out of fear of the demons they believed gained power over men through eating. The pagans fasted while mourning, believing that as long as the deceased's soul was near, a danger of demonic infection through eating and drinking was present. Fasting in the case of death amongst the Hebrews may have its roots in the belief in demons (Kittel, *Theological Dictionary of the New Testament*, 926-927), but this is unlikely.

46. Wimmer, *Fasting in the New Testament*, 10.

47. Berry, *Fasting Safely*, 4.

collected all the priests in the region, and on the third day after the fast was completed, he blessed some salt and mixed it with water after the manner of the Church and began to sprinkle in on the house, casting out a demon.[48] Many overseas missionaries relate their own stories about preparing themselves through fasting and prayer before performing exorcisms. Pastors might consider fasting before the many baptisms that they administer, an exorcism every Christian undergoes. But once again, it is not fasting itself that contains a secret power over the hidden hosts, but, rather, the one to whom fasting directs us: Jesus the victorious Christ. Fasting reminds us of our own intrinsic weakness, and points us to Christ, our strength.

> Fasting is the art of becoming hungry and thirsty. Hunger and thirst are always a signal that a being has started to decay and will not survive unless it receives reinforcement from outside in the form of food. In the Christian way, however, hunger and thirst are to be transformed into a quest for what is truly substantial for humans, for the food that does not perish[49]

Clearly, we triumph over the devil in fasting because it redirects our eyes from self and towards Jesus Christ as our "reinforcement from the outside". Yet the Church Fathers indicate that the greatest tactic of the devil against God's people was not fear, nor even lack of faith (although they may have been mistaken!). St. Jerome argues that fasting "prevents our thoughts from drawing us into the captivity of *lust*", conquering the devil of lust with "the humility that we have learned from Christ".[50] Conveyed, not only in these observations from St. Jerome but in many of the Church Fathers, is a special emphasis on the sin of lust as a particular avenue by which the devil tries to cause us to fall. Surprisingly, the Church Fathers spend more time talking about fasting as a way to attack the sin of lust than they do with respect to the sin of gluttony! This may merely reflect the personal struggles of the authors who shared a common experience as priests sworn to celibacy. Yet, sexual sins do stand in a special category of their own, especially when reflecting upon the words of St. Paul who makes a clear distinction between sexual sins that are sins against the Spirit and all other sorts of sins of the body (1 Cor 6:18). So too, there are undertones of this warning in the words of Paul encouraging us not to fall back into the sins of our youth (2 Tim 2:22; Ps 25:7). Accordingly, Luther broadens the efficaciousness of fasts for

---

48. Iberian Fathers, *Sayings of the Egyptian Fathers*, 129.
49. Papathanassiou, *Christian Fasting in Postmodern Society*, 268.
50. Jerome, *Homilies*, 94.

young people as one way, along with Scripture, prayer and working, which protects them from the "flames of lust."[51] Fasting disciplines the body by outwardly cutting off both lust and the opportunity for lust, the same things that faith does inwardly in the heart.[52] The power of lust may be the reason why St. Paul (who was a regular faster) advises the married Christians of Corinth to deprive themselves of sex for a time of prayer, in order to prevent the flesh from dominating Christian relationships (1 Cor 7:5).

Fasting certainly does distract us from temptations such as lust by helping us to focus on God and not the desires of our flesh [just like throwing oneself into a ditch full of ice, as was St. Francis' practice when sexually tempted[53]]. It is indisputable that the increased suffering and pain that fasting brings distracts us from many such passions[54] which seem to dominate the spirits of those of the male sex. A Desert Father was said to have burnt each of his ten fingers in the presence of a woman during a fast in an effort to battle temptation.[55] Although this may seem a bit "fanatical", it certainly is an effective means of diverting one's mind from lust. Commenting on the physiology of the practice, Doscorus said,

> now a monk must even transcend the law of nature and must certainly not fall into the slightest pollution of the flesh. On the contrary, he must mortify the flesh and not allow an excess of seminal fluid to accumulate. We should therefore try to keep the fluid depleted by the prolongation of fasting. Otherwise we arouse our sensual appetites.[56]

Fasting was understood to deplete the body of that which may cause us to sin. From a secular standpoint, one could then argue that fasting simply biologically decreases the sex drive. This may be true, but we cannot overlook the spiritual side. We are reminded in Luther's Galatians commentary in 1535 that fasting itself is not the source of victory, but the Spirit of our Lord is since,

> merely abstaining from food does not extinguish the heat of sexual desire by itself; but the Spirit must be added, that is, meditation

---

51. AE 4: 334.
52. AE 21:162.
53. Pelikan, *The Illustrated Jesus Through the Centuries*, 150.
54. Waddell, *The Desert Fathers*, 80.
55. Ibid., 82.
56. Russell, *The Lives of the Desert Fathers*, 105.

on the Word, faith and prayer. Fasting does indeed overcome the coarser outbursts of sexual desire; but the desires of the flesh themselves are conquered, not by an abstinence from food and drink, but by an earnest meditation on the Word and by the invocation of Christ.[57]

The power does not rest in the fast, but in the Lord, who looks favourably upon the fast, and graciously uses it to communicate His good work and share His victory with us.

---

57. AE 27: 92.

3

HUMBLING THE SOUL

WHAT IS IT ABOUT fasting, or, to capture the literal interpretation, "doing violence against one's body" and "chastising one's self", that makes it pleasant to a loving heavenly Father who, one would think, would wish His children to be happy and not miserable? It's a good question. Well, firstly, fasting is not an end in itself but a means to an end. He permits short term "pain" for long term "gain". After all, every father disciplines those he loves (Heb 12:6). And secondly, it is not so much what it does for *Him*, but what it does for *us* that makes it beneficial and even sacramental. As one protestant theologian puts it,

> The goal of any ascetic discipline is 'freedom'; we become more attendant of God and aware of our own inadequacies, contingencies and insufficiencies; and better listeners of God.[1]

Fasting changes us, not God. Someone once asked an Egyptian Church Father what fasts do. He replied, "They cause the soul to be humble. For it is written, 'behold my affliction and my suffering'" (Ps 24:18).[2]

> Through the embracing of the suffering and discomfort of fasting, Christians are positioned, furthermore, to deepen their understanding of the nature of suffering itself. First the pain of fasting reminds them of their nature and the choices that must be made

---

1. Towns, *Fasting for Spiritual Breakthrough*, 17.
2. Iberian Fathers, *Sayings of the Egyptian Fathers*, 17.

if they are to come not only to the fullness of their nature, but to the happiness promised them by their creation. Second, one's pain and suffering lose their seeming futility as they are united to the pain and suffering of Christ. For in fasting one is faced solidly with the fragility of human nature and is reminded of the need for one's redemption and of the suffering that was experience by Christ for the sake of our redemption. [Then] [i]n one's own small way, one contributes, in one's suffering, to the aid and redemption of others, in the same way that prayer, good works, and almsgiving contribute to the sanctification of the people of God.[3]

The bitter herbs of fasting humble *us*, exposing the sinners that we really are, inside—in spite of the seeming assets of our wealth, health and personal success—and how deeply our lives depend on the Creator. It is only when we acknowledge our dependence upon God and His provision for our basic needs that we become aware of His provision for our many non-physical needs. Fasting is as much an expression of despondency and affliction as other more familiar forms of contrition and repentance.[4] Each one directs us out of ourselves and into God. For first we must be convinced that there is nothing good that resides within us—no one "does good, not even one" (Ps 14:3)—in even the tiniest pockets of our lives and hearts. Fasting draws attention to these details. God gives us food, and yet we forget. We take for granted the "daily bread" with which God continues to feed us and all people. Well, the more we recognize how we already trust God with the little things in life, appreciating the wonderful ways in which He abundantly provides food for our hungry stomachs, the more we will learn to trust Him for greater miracles.[5] And we may even come to discover that those "little things" are, in fact, the greatest of miracles, as almighty God continues to hide Himself in a bowl of water, a cup of wine, and a piece of bread, for us and our salvation. Conflicting with our natural inclinations that demand of God the things which we do not possess, confusing our real needs with our perceived needs (which incidentally are often disguises for our *wants*), fasting teaches us to be content in life with what God has already given us. By delaying the satisfaction of these desires,[6] we are liberated to desire the

3. Loughlin, *Thomas Aquinas and the importance of fasting to the Christian life*, 356.

4. Lambert, *Fasting as a Penitential Rite*, 490.

5. Iberian Fathers, *Fathers of the Church*, 32.

6. Adalbert de Vogüé, *The Rule of Saint Benedict: Doctrinal and Spiritual Commentary*, 235.

things of God. The seventeenth-century Lutheran mystic and theologian, Johann Arndt (1555-1621) argues that

> Christians do not have their lusts in earthly food, but their internal eye is directed to the eternal food. Christians do not strut about with earthly clothes but look to their heavenly clothing of the glory of God, and their glorified bodies.[7]

In fasting our eyes look up to God, our clothes are changed by Christ, as God rearranges our priorities and reveals to us our real needs, ridding our minds of all our perceived needs. For instance, we sinners have a real need to be shepherded by God. Yet his dominion is often undermined by the passions of our flesh. When the flesh is not subdued, we allow it to control us, robbing the Lord of the throne which belongs to Him alone. Fasting opens the door of our heart to the Holy Spirit who works to put the Lord Jesus "first" in our lives. Of course, He remains enthroned in the heart of every Christian, having usurped that position from the enemy at the moment of Holy Baptism. Yet our old self and old Adam do their very best to hoist Him off by our rebellion. Which is why, even though baptized once, we must drown all of our sins daily in those same old baptismal waters. Humility unlocks that gate granting us passage to that incoming flood of cleansing grace. With the force of a tidal wave surpassing the strongest tsunami imaginable, the filthy rags of our pride and sin are ripped off of our mortal bodies, leaving us naked and exposed, and, thus, well prepared to be dressed in the spotless clothing of Christ's righteous robe of grace and immortality. In the spirit of II Chronicles 7:14f, fasting is the "best way to help meet the conditions of humility".[8] Fasting and humility go hand in hand. Have you ever pulled over the car to the side of the road in order to splash some icy cold water on your face when falling asleep at the wheel, after becoming far too comfortable—dangerously comfortable—as a driver on your journey? Fasting has an equally humbling effect on our spirits, awakening them to take heed of their perilous condition. And either we do it ourselves, or God will do it for us. By choosing not to fast we resist the Holy Spirit's work in our lives, compelling God to humble us in other ways. It is far better to be humbled by our own hands than have almighty God humble us by His hand. Fasting does more than merely destroy the idol of food (Deut 32:15) and help control this Western addiction by fighting the

---

7. Arndt, *True Christianity*, 91.
8. Towns, *Fasting for Spiritual Breakthrough*, 8.

sin of gluttony (Prov 23:1-8). It helps to empty ourselves of ourselves and henceforth make room for God and the Gospel that He brings.

The gift of fasting causes us to hunger so that we can be fed at times when we may have not noticed our spiritual hunger pangs:

> He humbled you, causing you to hunger and then feeding you with manna . . . to teach you that man does not live on bread alone but on every word that proceeds from the mouth of God (Deut 8:3).

Only with a healthy appetite does food taste delicious: human food and divine food. It is only when we are weakened that God can strengthen us, when we are "bowed down" that God will raise us (Ps 146:8), when we are emptied that God can fill us up: emptied by the Law and filled by the Gospel. Certainly, food still nourishes even when we consume it without feeling any hunger. This is the case with the food from our kitchen tables and the food from the Lord's table. Yet although food's efficacy is not contingent upon our sentiments or experiences, our appreciation for its necessity is. We can learn something profound from secular nutritionists and dieticians who remind us that "we eat better when we eat slow". Slow and even "reflective" eating is better for our digestion. The mystic Catherine of Siena (1347-1380), one of the few women granted the title "Doctor" of the Roman Catholic Church, contemplated a conversation with God concerning our "spiritual digestion" through repentance in *The Dialogue* saying:

> no sooner is your vessel emptied than it is filled. For nothing can remain empty. Just so, the heart is a vessel that cannot remain empty. Emptied of worldly pleasures, it is filled with the divine love of the Crucified Christ . . . [allowing you] to rest in a sea of peace.[9]

Likewise, Jesus decided to demonstrate His power to fill the world with His bread amongst four thousand *hungry* people (Matt 15:32; Mark 8:2,3)! The mystical devotional writer, Catherine of Genoa (1448-1510) is a model of this interplay. She actively sought,

> to destroy all self-love, at whatever the cost, so that she might be filled by the divine love. This transformation required an ever more rigorous self-discipline. She practised extraordinary fasting and experienced extraordinary spiritual consolation, but she was

---

9. Catherine of Siena, *The Dialogue*, 109.

neither exhausted by the one nor exalted by the other. She avoided public notice in all her many acts of charity.[10]

Her experience may not be our own. We should be careful to follow the example of the saints—especially the mystics—for the wrong reasons. Sadly, many Christians hunger to "have" an experience with God or to "feel" His presence in an extraordinary way, dissatisfied with the nourishment of the Means of Grace as their spiritual diet (John 6:48-58). Instead, what we learn from this sister in Christ, is that when we are emptied of ourselves, we are filled by God, and this is a far better condition in which to be, however painful the process. In agreement, Luther's exposition of Psalm 109:24 exposes our weakness outside of Christ "who is the living bread and oil of the saints". When our "knees are weakened" then "the face of the church" is beautiful[11] and ready to feed on the Word of the Gospel. In addressing the misconception that fasting was penal in character, Thomas Aquinas argued that fasting ought to also be sought for its

> "cooling" or sobering effect upon one's person, something that makes one fit to contemplate these higher or heavenly things better, or, at the very least, to pursue one's intellectual studies more freely. In a word, fasting helps greatly to reduce, and possibly even eliminate, the perturbations that afflict one's person.[12]

Scholar Stephen Loughlin continues his reflection by underscoring the fact that Aquinas and the catholic Church understood fasting as a tool in preparing followers of Jesus to better appreciate divine nourishment through the seasons of the Church and to appropriately prepare themselves for the reception of her wonderful gifts:

> The times for fasting are set with an eye to those seasons within a church's liturgical year where its members are called to raise their sight to heavenly things and seek forgiveness for their sins. Thus, before the celebration of major liturgical feasts, Christians are called to a devout preparation that importantly includes fasting; again, the mind is set most sharply to consider these most high things, the appetite is drawn away from other goods and set upon the highest good, and the comportment of the person before God is addressed properly through fasting. Thomas notes that the

---

10. Jones, *The Study of Spirituality*, 313.
11. AE 11: 357-358.
12. Loughlin, *Thomas Aquinas and the importance of fasting to the Christian life*, 348.

season of Lent is an especially important time to fast. He also includes fasting in the preparations one makes before receiving the sacraments, particularly baptism, the Eucharist, and ordination, where both the priest-to-be and the people whom he will serve are called to fast, so that they will be ready to receive and enjoy most fully and appropriately this great gift.[13]

There is thus also a highly practical element to this kind of fasting in context of our great need to be fed by God and His Word. We are free to feed on the Word when we are not distracted by the carnal appetite.[14] Fasting abstains from eating, preventing the interruption of prayer. In the *Sayings of the Fathers*, we hear how many of the Desert Fathers would not eat that which needed to be cooked, not only to practice a simple diet, but also because cooking takes time, time that could be spent in prayer.[15] Some have argued that giving one's time to God in the silence of prayer is much greater than giving Him your wealth and tithes because in our Western society, time has become the most valuable good. For this reason, because of the value that society places on "good eating" and "precious time", today's hunger-strike is an example of the secularization of a religious practice.[16] While changing society is an honourable cause, lasting change must begin with self.

St. John of the Cross (1542-1591), a Spanish Carmelite, one of the great mystical writers of the sixteenth century, from whom even the Pope sought guidance, writes,

> the soul in this condition ... is like those who are sick, who are extremely tired and having lost their taste and appetite, find all food nauseating and everything a disturbance and annoyance. In everything they think about one desire, desire for [spiritual] health, and all that does not lead to health is a bother to them.[17]

Apparently for some fasters—and I cannot include myself in this category as fasting never ceases to be painful to me ... sigh—they can come to a point in which their hunger pangs are no longer burdensome and, instead, help them to focus solely upon their spiritual nourishment. Some mystics even claimed that spiritual nourishment sufficed in granting them the energy required to physically survive their fast. For instance, because our

---

13. Ibid., 350.
14. Russell, *The Lives of the Desert Fathers*, 23.
15. Ibid., 71.
16. Reijnen, *Fasting – Some Protestant Remarks "Not by Bread Alone"*, 277.
17. John of the Cross, *Selected Writings*, 227.

Lord's Body and Blood also offer physical health (1 Cor 11:30), some Desert Fathers would restrict themselves to a diet which contained solely the Eucharist. When we can say that all we really desire in life is the Word, then, according to the Desert Fathers, we have truly been made perfect:[18] we have been changed.

In fasting, we are not made perfect—the Church Fathers are not always right: due to our human frailty we continue to fall—but we are indeed changed. "Our soul is like wax, whatever a man impresses upon it, it holds that image".[19] Fasting is a means of softening that wax, preparing it for the print of the image of God. Yet fasting without humility is vain and useless. Some argue that the most prominent feature of fasting, and unique to the Old Testament, is the fact that fasting expresses submission to God, as the phrase "self-mortification" and "self-humbling" indicates.[20] The fast is an act of self-renunciation and self-discipline which is designed to "make an impression on God, to mollify His wrath and to move him to grant what man desires".[21] Thus, the Christian fasts when he hopes that God will liberate him from tormenting care. The entire population fasts in times or emergency in hopes that God may turn aside the calamity. Prayer and fasting go hand in hand to cause God to answer.[22] In fact, fasting is hardly ever recorded in the Holy Scriptures as occurring without prayer.

Fasting reminds us that we are sinners who stand before God, and of our great dependence on Him, helping us to better value the Gospel. God would have us become dogs, who after sniffing an empty dish, remember the hand that feeds us (Matt 15:27). And the hungrier the stomach, the deeper the appreciation. The greater the sin, the greater the grace; the greater the impression/experience of sin in my life, the greater the impression/experience of grace in my life. Fasting mystically intensifies this experience of sin. It is sacramental in that it *prepares us* for a state of being filled by God in general and filled by His forgiveness and grace in particular. Fasting, in a sense, makes room for God's Spirit, who brings forgiveness by purging us of the pride that prevents us from confessing our sin and receiving God's grace. Plainly put, it helps us to repent! When approached from

---

18. Waddell, *The Desert Fathers*, 127.
19. Arndt, *True Christianity*, 98.
20. Kittel, *The Theological Dictionary of the New Testament*, 927.
21. Ibid.
22. Ibid.

this perspective, a fundamental connection with fasting and repentance becomes obvious. A Jewish Rabbi states:

> The confession we make with our lips is a beginning. The penance we inflict upon our bodies through fasting, leads us along further still toward the acknowledgement that we have sinned against ourselves and others.[23]

Fasting as a way of allowing ourselves to be disciplined by God is a natural expression of repentance, a "sign of love,"[24] practiced alongside contrition and prayer for forgiveness. If the sacraments can be described as "celebrations of salvation,"[25] then fasting is a preparation for that celebration.

God teaches us something profound and perplexing about ourselves in fasting. The Law is at work in its entirety, so that the priceless Gospel can have even greater effect. It highlights and emphasizes the bad news in order to increase the "experience" of the good news. Simply put, "[t]he Gospel is good news because it always changes a bad situation".[26] Through the sacraments we affirm that there is nothing more desirable in the sight of God than to be what he has intended us to be,[27] affirming our hunger to be filled by God. When we are weak, then we are made strong (2 Cor 6:5). Fasting as an expression of repentance is God's way of better preparing us for the reception of the Gospel.[28] Incidentally, the saints advise us to

---

23. Knobel, *Jewish Fasts: Gates of the Seasons*, 50.
24. Wimmer, *Fasting in the New Testament*, 117.
25. Elliott, *The Christ Life*, 24.
26. Ibid., 43.
27. Ibid., 45.
28. It is vital that fasting as a means to this end is properly understood. It helps to answer that troubling question about how a loving God can approve of self-inflicted pain whether manifested in fasting or the simple tears of a penitent heart. Penitent actions and expressions of remorse which follow absolution, instead of preceding it, are displeasing and insulting to God, defaming His work and labelling Him a liar by doubting His Gospel promise. Yet where these actions do not follow holy absolution but appropriately precede the absolution they are useful in contrition. This is incidentally why fasting precedes the Eucharist instead of following it. The communicants should be encouraged to leave the Supper rejoicing and not with solemn faces of remorse. So, too, the Reformation debate over private confession and absolution pivoted around the question of "penance" which suggested that forgiveness was not free, and not grace, but conditional upon the penitent's acts and prayers that followed it. Still today, in the rite of private confession and absolution, the focus remains on the work of God in absolution instead of the work of man in confession. Therefore, the faithful ought to make use of this gift frequently, even if they do not have any particularly heavy or burdensome sins to confess. It provides an

meditate on the Scriptures while fasting[29] since the strength and energy to fast is drawn from such divine contemplation.[30] By fasting and repentance, we bring our dark inner condition into the light where God can easily haul it away, while at the same time preventing us from committing other venial sins (like gluttony, lust, etc.) during the process of this repentance. As the popular devotional writer and Cistercian Abbot, St. Bernard of Clairvaux (1090-1153) spoke,

> An overflowing sewer contaminates the whole house with intolerable filth. It is vain for you to empty it when the filth is still flooding in, to repent while you do not cease to sin.[31]

Although, according to our Old Adam and original sin, the stench of our sin surrounds us until we are freed from it through a Christian death, the aroma of Christ, emanating from our new Adam, overpowers that odour. It is, in fact, the pleasing fragrance of God (2 Cor 2:15). A repentance that is not governed by a desire to cease from sin—in spite of our lack of "success" in completely overcoming any particular sin—is hypocritical. True fasting then is, in the words of Eastern St. Chrysostom (347-407), "fasting from sin" (St. Chrysostom, 1963, 80-81), "abstaining from all sinful desires" (I Peter 2:11). This kind of fasting is accessible to all believers for it characterizes the life of the Christian. It is synonymous with repentance. The great reformer and patriarch of Constantinople continues:

> For it is possible for someone not fasting to fast. How is this? I shall tell you. While on the one hand we are taking food, let us, on the other, abstain from sin . . . . I used to hear many a man say he found it difficult to endure the burden of want of food, and blame the weakness of his body, and utter many other bitter laments, saying that his health was being ruined because he had to go without a bath and had to confine his drinking to water. No such excuse is possible with regards to the fasting from sin.[32]

---

intimate, one-on-one encounter with Jesus, who seeks to fill us with good things even when we do not feel particularly hungry.

29. Iberian Fathers, *Fathers of the Church*, 122.

30. Adalbert de Vogüé, *The Rule of Saint Benedict: Doctrinal and Spiritual Commentary*, 234.

31. Bernard of Clairvaux, *Selected Works*, 73.

32. Chrysostom, *Baptismal Instructions*, 80-81.

What can we give to God that he does not have? A fast is an appropriate gift when offered from a heart of "praise and thanksgiving."[33] Although God "does not delight in sacrifice" nor is He "pleased with burnt offerings", "the sacrifices of God are a broken spirit; a broken and contrite heart [He] will not despise" (Ps 51: 16-17). God despises fasting as an end in itself but rejoices in fasting insofar as it presents to Him this frail and contrite heart.

As a means of repentance, the Hebrews normally associated fasting with mourning or lamenting for either some public or private calamity (2 Sam 1:12;12:16) be it present or impending. There are only three occurrences of fasting in the Psalter, each time displaying a lament for an individual (Ps 35:13;69:10;109:24). Thus, Old Testament fasting was often practiced as a sign of sorrow, as in the ritual of mourning, and less of an ascetic practice[34] which it became for the early Church and remains today. In I Kings 21:27, Ahab demonstrates the sincerity of his confession by tearing his clothes, putting on sackcloth and fasting before God while repenting over Jezebel's sin. God recognized his genuine humility and forgave him.

Fasting amplifies our internal feelings of remorse over sin.[35] In fasting we visually confess with our bodies what we verbally confess with our mouths. *What* we are and *who* we are is *felt* in fasting. The sacraments do not merely wipe clean our dirty slates but are a constant reminder of who we are in Christ.[36] Thomas Aquinas challenges us to understand fasting not simply as a means of self-discipline, but also as something that

> reminds Christians of their status in the order of creation, of the comportment that they should take before their Creator, of the joy and self-possession that are promised to the moderate, and how distinct Christians are from the rest of the world insofar as fasting serves a profound statement of their faith in, and hope and love of, God.[37]

The faster is intensely reminded of this position within the created order in his physical hunger pains (i.e., a reminder of one's mortal body is a reminder of God's immortal body to which one is joined). Fasting contributes to our awareness of our status as sinners, while the sacraments contribute to

---

33. AE 21: 155.
34. McKenzie, *Second Isaiah*, 165.
35. Towns, *Fasting for Spiritual Breakthrough*, 25.
36. Elliott, *The Christ Life*, 29.
37. Loughlin, *Thomas Aquinas and the importance of fasting to the Christian life*, 344.

our awareness of our status as saints.[38] Our unworthiness as sinners, the filth and dirt in our lives, *appears* visually in our sackcloth and ashes and malnourished faces: our hearts are worn on our sleeves. Often it takes the use of all of our five senses (all five are evident in fasting) to truly become aware of our sin and our position before God as sinners. When we truly fear God and reflect upon what God's judgement of our sin implies, it is difficult not to fast while in a state of repentance. In 1 Sam 28:20 Saul would not eat in his repentant state. Fasting conjoined with repentance not only *produces* good fruits of faith, but *is* a fruit of faith.[39]

Unsurprisingly, due to its interdependence with repentance, there is a definite mournful dimension to some fasts. As discussed earlier, Luther did not care much for this kind of fasting and occasionally insisted that fasting should be joyful, reacting against the mandatory, coerced fasts of the medieval Catholics, especially the forty day Lenten fast ("Fastenzeit" or "fasting time" in German).[40] Similarly, Zechariah 8:18-19, advocates that there be only cheerful feasts remembering how God honoured past promises.[41] Reflecting on the Ember Days (*Quattuor tempora*) of the Lenten season, Tertullian questioned whether or not fasting was at all appropriate since the baptized should rejoice in gratitude while reflecting upon their salvation.[42] Such comments cannot be taken out of context. They suggest practical solutions to well known incidents of misuse and abuse of God's gifts. We fast when the bridegroom is absent, in sorrow and *in joy*, both joy in the second coming and joy in His continual multi-faceted real presence amongst us. Therefore, even a mournful fast of repentance is inherently joyful as it proclaims not only the helplessness of man, but also the sovereignty and mercy of God who hears our prayer. Thus, in Christian fasting there is unquestionably only room for, in the words of St. Augustine, a "joyful faster".[43]

---

38. Ibid., 48.
39. AP: XII.
40. However, Luther did recognize the mournful fast as legitimate when done with the correct motivation: "We often read that when people were fasting, they put on sackcloth and strewed ashes on their heads, the way the King of Nineveh did together with the whole city (Jonah 3:5-6). But that was another kind of fasting, when they learned from their need and misery" (AE 21: 156).
41. AE 29: 278.
42. Wimmer, *Fasting in the New Testament*, 31.
43. Augustine, *Sermons for Christmas and Epiphany*, 130.

And because Christians "[r]ejoice with those who rejoice, [and] weep with those who weep" (Rom 12:15) this function of fasting, as something coupled with repentance, is intended for both individual and *group* use.[44] In Biblical times, fasting was both an act of *individual* lamentation and penance, and a *communal* rite of mourning and confession during periods of collective crisis and affliction.[45] When the trouble is communal, so is the fast. In Isaiah 58 the "trumpet call" was used to announce to the people the beginning of a solemn day of fasting and summon them all to worship. Likewise, when the sin is communal, so is the fast. Communal fasts were often demanded by the prophets, priests and kings in the Hebraic world. Although they need to be done for the right reasons and with the right motivations, in a spirit of humility, as indicated in Matthew 6:16-18, they do achieve good things.[46] And so, Luther

> could nor would introduce such fasting unless it had been agreed harmoniously beforehand. You see, in this way the Christian Church would have plenty of fasting to do, and no one would have the right to accuse us of despising and completely rejecting the practice of fasting.[47]

The blowing of the *shofar* would signal the beginning of these fasts during stressful times (like during droughts, plague, siege, etc.) in order to inspire repentance.[48] The prophet Jonah recounts the king proclaiming a

44. I have included here a complete list of corporate fasts which include those for repentance purposes: Israel at Mizpah (1 Sam 7:6); Saul's army (1 Sam 14:24); men of Jabesh Gilead fasting the death of Saul (1 Sam 31:11-13; 1 Chron 10:11-12); the men of David fasting and mourning the death of Saul and Jonathan (2 Sam 1:12); Judah asking for wisdom and help before battle (2 Chron 20: 3,4); people of Nineveh in fear of God's judgement (Jonah 3:5-9); the remnant of Israel returning after the captivity pray for safety (Ezra 8:21-23); a communal public confession of sin with sackcloth and ashes (Neh 9:1); the kings decree brought mourning, weeping and lamenting (Esther 4:3); for Esther's safety (Esther 4:15,16); the Pharisees (Matt 9:14; Mk 2:18; Lk 5:33); the disciples of John the Baptizer (Matt 9:14; Mk 2:18; Lk 5:33); the multitudes following Jesus (Matt 15:32; Mk 8:2-3); and the Jews committed to killing Paul (Acts 23:12-23) (Towns, *Fasting for Spiritual Breakthrough*, 4).

45. Koehler, 1996, 1012.

46. Some despise group fasts because of Jesus' summon of them to be private. Yet again, Jesus warned about the publicity of the fast for the sake of drawing attention to oneself and thereby earning pious favour in the eyes of men. There is a time and a place for all things, evaluated according to context and motivation.

47. AE 21:160.

48. Bloch, *The Biblical and Historical background of Jewish Customs and Ceremonies*, 147.

national fast of repentance, weeping and lamenting to the heathen people of Nineveh (Jonah 3:4-13). The fast was more than a symbolic turning away from wicked ways towards the living God, consisting of an assembly of individuals confessing their private sins in a communal fashion. The nation fasted together. God heard the cry of these sinners and had mercy. Likewise, Samuel assembled all of Israel at Mitzpah and they all fasted and confessed their sins by drawing out water and pouring it out before the Lord, symbolizing the pouring out of one's heart in repentance and humility (1 Sam 7:6). In Joel 1:13-14, the priests called for a corporate fast since the entire nation needed to repent for contributing to the ruin of their nation by their sins, resulting in their desperate situation. The call for a communal fast demanded that all people fast and pray by giving up what they were doing and going to the temple to cry out to the Lord. Everyone was called to return to the Lord with "fasting, weeping and mourning" (Joel 2:12).

In this Scripture from the Prophet Joel, we find fasting affixed not only to repentance, but also to mourning as a natural and heart-felt outpouring of grief. Have you ever attempted to weep and eat at the same time? It is next to impossible. The "outpour of tears is inimical to the intake of food".[49] Genuine national mourning was often accompanied by national fasting in the Old Testament. In Nehemiah 9:1 fasting and repentance translated into wearing sackcloth and spreading dust on heads. When the Philistines killed Saul, the people fasted seven days (1 Sam 31:11-13). David called a fast in mourning over the death of Abner, and its seriousness is demonstrated by David calling a curse down on anyone who failed to observe the fast (2 Sam 3:31-35). 1 Chron 10: 11-12 recounts the fasting of the nation while mourning for the deceased Saul. In the words of the Psalmist, "My tears have become my bread day and night" (Ps 41:4). It is as normal to fast in sorrow or trouble, as it is to curl up into the "cradle position" while in passionate mourning, or dropping down onto the knees, hands folded and eyes shut tight, when intensely praying. Although kneeling, genuflecting, prostrating and other reverent gestures during the Divine Service of the Church may be *adiaphora* and left to personal choice, the more the worshipper appreciates what is actually happening in that space and at that time, the more he will be inclined to change his physical gestures at key moments during the holy liturgy. Our bodily posture is rarely neutral. And believing heaven is meeting with earth in the Mass moves our bodies to mirror that which the Holy Spirit is already working in our hearts and souls.

---

49. Lambert, *Fasting as a Penitential Rite*, 484.

> When the heart is bowed down, fasting is a proper expression of its feelings. Who cares to eat at all, or more than a little, when he is greatly depressed?[50]

It is not surprising that Saul, blinded by the Lord in Acts 9:9, fasted. The people of Moab, in devastation over ruin, wailed and fasted (Isa 15:1-4). Because of concern for his fellow soldiers, Uriah fasted (2 Sam 11:11). David "humbled his soul with fasting" even for the illness of his enemies (Ps 35:13)! Jonathan would not eat out of grief for David who was about to be disgraced and killed by Saul (1 Sam 20:34). This natural expression of sorrow in Jonathan gained God's attention since "fasting, weeping, and mourning" are all "external signs of repentance".[51]

Accordingly, the *ritual of mourning* resembled the *ritual of repentance* both in thought and practice; the faster physically looked and felt like the mourner as the faster often adopted the attitude of a mourner.[52] Similarly, both rituals recognized the reality of man's mortality due to human sinfulness. Naturally then, fasting was intermingled with prayer as well; the two fit together nicely. In Isaiah 58 we hear the Israelites complain that God has not 'seen' their fast nor 'heard' their prayer. The prayer was packaged in the faster's contrite heart, seen visually in his contrite body. We all know how hard it is to articulate pain in words. "Fasting shares in the dialogical nature of prayer".[53] Fasting naturally flows into prayer, petitions, and even complaints, as characterized by the laments of the Psalms.[54]

When we fast, we demonstrate that we sincerely 'mean' our repentance; it is, in other words, the package of a prayer. Neither prayer nor repentance are semi-Gnostic intellectual experiences, belonging to the sphere of mind alone, but are rather entire body and soul experiences. Why else do tears accompany our prayers at times, or do we drop to our knees when pleading for mercy? When we are truly contrite, we cry; when we are truly repentant, we fast: two actions which involve the entire body. The intimate union of the body and soul and their harmonious act of repentance is eloquently articulated by St. Bernard of Clairvaux:

---

50. Lenski, *Interpretation of St. Matthew's Gospel*, 369.
51. AE 18:96.
52. Kittel, *The Theological Dictionary of the New Testament*, 927.
53. Lambert, Fasting as a Penitential Rite, 480
54. Ibid., 487.

> Truly that will be a most dreadful return and eternal wretchedness, when [the body] can no longer repent or do penance. For where there is no body there is no possibility of action (Matt 24:28). Where there is no action, no satisfaction can be made. Accordingly, to repent is to grieve; to do penance is a remedy for sorrow. He who has no hands cannot lift his heart in his hands to heaven (Lam 3:41). He who has not come to himself before the death of the flesh must remain trapped in himself for eternity.[55]

Johann Arndt argues that repentance cannot be understood outside of the mortification of the flesh:

> Through repentance, the mortification and crucifixion of the flesh and all fleshly lusts and evil qualities of the heart and the life-giving power of the Spirit comes . . . The two things are tied together. The new life and the renewal of the spirit follow upon the mortification of the flesh. When the old man dies the new comes to life and when the new comes to life the old dies . . . The mortification of the flesh must occur through true repentance.[56]

The fact that sin is an act not just of the mind or just of the body, but is the unified activity of one person (who is both body and soul), and that penance is thus both a mind and body experience, is often overlooked by Christians today. Arndt goes on to argue that the old Adam did not become corrupt in the Fall in just a spiritual/intellectual way, but also in an earthy, fleshly way. And so this "twisted, evil quality of man" must be changed through repentance and by the "mortification of the flesh".[57] Because "Christ redeems the *whole* person" . . . let us "beg forgiveness for our sins of the heart with our lips, and the sins of our bodies by our fasting".[58]

Shocking to Christians who seek a "Prosperity Gospel" that promises temporal health, wealth and happiness, St. John of the Cross welcomed

---

55. Bernard of Clairvaux, *Selected Works*, 71.
56. Arndt, *True Christianity*, 41.
57. Ibid.
58. Ibid. Arndt continues: "Out of [repentance or true conversion] are awakened in his heart repentance and sorrow. From the Gospel, however, he understands God's grace and through faith he receives forgiveness for his sins in Christ. Through this repentance, the mortification and crucifixion of the flesh and all fleshly lusts and the evil qualities of the heart and the life-giving power of the spirit comes . . . The two are tied together. The new life and the renewal of the spirit follow upon the mortification of the flesh." Thus, in comments on Galatians 5:24, "Those who belong to Christ have crucified the flesh with its passions and desires". (Ibid)

fasting as an experience of 'spiritual darkness'. The "night" of fasting signifies a deprivation of the gratification of the soul's appetites:

> Just as night is nothing but the privation of light and, consequently, of all objects visible by means of the light (darkness and emptiness, then, for the faculty of sight) the mortification of the appetites can be called a night for the soul. To deprive one of the gratifications of the appetites in all things is like living in darkness and in void. The eye feeds on its objects by means of light in such a way that when the light is extinguished the eye no longer sees them. Similarly do people by means of their faculties feed and pasture on worldly things that gratify their faculties. When the appetites are extinguished (or mortified) one no longer feeds on the pleasure of these things, but lives in a void and in darkness with respect to appetites.[59]

The body and soul must experience these times of darkness in order to fully appreciate the light that enlightens them. After all, Christianity is the continual death of self. There is, after all, no resurrection without crucifixion. How do we confess our crucified Saviour if we only carry the message upon our lips? It seems somewhat unauthentic. In our Western materialistic society, whose god is in the business of selling experiences of success and glory, we Christians are tempted to hide the wounds that the Lord has given us to bear (Gal 6:17). On the value of bodily mortification, Tertullian writes with obvious sarcastic undertones:

> Well is it fitting that we beg pardon for sin in scarlet and purple? Come, then, bring a pin to part the hair and powder to polish the teeth and scissors to trim the nails and, if any meretricious beauty, any artificial bloom may be had, hasten and apply it to the lips or cheeks! . . . Multiply expenses, search for the rich, gross flesh of fatted fowls, refine old wine and, if anyone should ask you why you make good cheer, then say to him: "I have sinned against the Lord. I am in danger of perishing forever. Therefore am I now weakened and wasted and tormented, so that I may win for myself the pardon of God whom I have injured by my sin?"[60]

Similarly St. Cyprian (200-258), who chose to live in poverty, writes,

> [A]re we to believe that a man is sorrowing with all his heart, that he is calling on the Lord with fasting, tears and lamentations, when

---

59. John of the Cross, *Selected Writings*, 64.
60. Tertullian, *Treatise on Penance*, 34.

> from the very day of his sin he is found daily at the baths . . . . when he goes about laughing cheerfully, how can he be lamenting the state of death he is in? . . . Is he courting someone's favour when he is out of favour with God?[61]

The purpose of fasting as lament is best articulated in these poetic and poignant words of David:

> Yet when they were ill, I put on sackcloth and humbled myself with fasting. When my prayers returned to me unanswered, I went about mourning as though for my friend or brother. I bowed my head in grief as though weeping for my mother (Psalm 35:13-14).

The physical behaviour of the faster visually displays the spiritual countenances of repentance and affliction, as reflected in the emotive language of the Psalmist. After all, the Psalms are the songs of the crucified and risen Christ, spoken by Him, through us. *This* is the cry of the fasting David. *This* is the cry of the fasting Christ. *This* is the cry of each and every fasting Christian.

---

61. Cyprian, *The Lapsed*, 37.

4

Fasting and Prayer

David's words in Psalm 35:13 illustrate how the fabric of fasting, humility and repentance are intricately interwoven in creating one distinct tapestry. They also reveal a correlative relationship between *prayer* and fasting through repentance. Repentance is a form of prayer when a confession of sin—which trusts in a God who is generous and merciful in offering absolution to His beloved children for the sake of His Son—governs, drives and shapes it. Yet this Psalm introduces petitionary prayer for the needs of others as another reason to fast, since David fasted specifically for the illness of his enemies. Fasting, then, is not limited to expressions of repenting or mourning. It is also a natural way of uplifting the cares and concerns of ourselves and our neighbours in prayer. Fasting, repentance and prayer have this in common: they are the humble cry of God's needy children before their heavenly Father. The Psalms are the prayers of Jesus as they echo through the cruciform shape of the Christian life. The tears of penance, sorrow, and hardship are expressed in the lips of the praying Christian, as we pray in Jesus' name. The petition packaged in the body of the faster is offered as a gift to God, as we approach with faith in Jesus. Almighty God possesses everything already, except our sins, troubles and "broken hearts" (Ps 51:17). As mind-boggling as this is, this good and gracious King wants them all! The fasting from Christ's cross was evident in those holy last words: "I thirst". Christ thirsted for our sins, burdens, and cares, in order to release us from them. He lifted them off of our shoulders, placing them on His own, and carried them off to heaven Himself. He fasted for us; we fast for others. Fasting remains His means for us to bring the petitions that weigh us down, before His heavenly throne.[1] God answers Daniel's cry "because of [his] prayer" (Dan 10:12). "Though there is no explicit mention of prayer. Fasting presumed the presence of prayer. Fasting constitutes something of a synecdoche for prayer; mere mention of fasting implies the presence of prayer as well".[2]

The Old Testament is filled with accounts of fasting occurring while praying for specific concerns. Ezra fasted before a long trip for the safety of himself and the others travelling with him (Ezra 8:21-23). Esther fasted for direction: for three days she fasted in preparation for the discerning of a life-changing decision, in order to receive God's help before confronting the king (Esther 4:6-16). In 2 Chron 20:3-4, Jehosophat proclaimed a national fast in light of the attacks of the enemy nations as a way of seeking help and guidance from the Lord.[3] King Darius fasted for Daniel that he would be spared from the jaws of the lions (Dan 6:18). Hannah in 1 Sam 1:7-8 grieved her childlessness and wept and fasted and prayed for children. The prayers of God's people are characteristically coupled with fasting. In fact, affliction and fasting go hand in hand with hands folded, or, rather, gripped in prayer appealing to the mercy of God. In the Hebrew, "afflicted person" is often treated synonymously with those fasting.[4] After all, petitionary prayer usually arises from a state of affliction or crisis, and crisis occurs on account of sin. Therefore, fasting is driven by the acknowledgement of one's affliction as a consequence of one's own deeds. Yet Christian fasting includes remorse and a repentance that appeals to divine mercy. Unlike other religions where there is great uncertainty as to how merciful the deity actually is and will respond, "in Christ, the son of God, we already have an answer due to His promise. Old Testament laments including physical manifestations like fasting, allude to the mercy of God."[5]

Fasting demonstrates the sincerity of the prayer and the importance of our appeal. Hannah fasted in constant sorrow. Her fasting embodied her intense desire for God to grant her a child (1 Sam 1). Jacob's wrestling with the Angel of the Lord, refusing to let go until He blessed him, is a

---

1. Waddell, *The Desert Fathers*, 17.
2. Lambert, *Fasting as a Penitential Rite*, 491.
3. Towns, *Fasting for Spiritual Breakthrough*, 74.
4. Lambert, *Fasting as a Penitential Rite*, 484.
5. Ibid, 481.

courageous and honourable example of faith, demonstrating the importance he placed in God's precious promise (Gen 32: 22-31). Fasting communicates the seriousness of the problem and the greatness of the answer.[6] As a Jewish rabbi once observed,

> Man cannot force God to yield to him. God should however, in his great loving-kindness, yield to the prayer of a man who humiliates himself before him.[7]

Though less 'presumptuous', in his comments on Paul's First Epistle to the Corinthians Luther also advises that, "strong prayer should always be accompanied by strong fasting".[8] Our changeless God offers the gift of fasting to all of us today as a sacramental way of making our needs known, so that He can meet them.

The danger inherent in associating fasting with prayer—namely describing fasting as something that strengthens our prayers before God—is that it may become an inadvertent attempt to manipulate God. Examples of God's people unwittingly caving into temptations of this sort are endless. Incidentally, the error of focusing on our works instead of God's was one of the troubles with the fasts of the Israelites in Isaiah 58 [see Appendix I]. Fasting is not about "trying to get something out of God". 'Religions of the Law' highlight the role of the self as they expect to receive something from God for their sacrifices. For them fasting functions as a formula for personal reward. The 'Religion of the Gospel' focuses on God's work and not ours.

Commenting on Zechariah 7:1-6, Luther argues that we actually fast for our own pleasure instead of God's whenever we trust in our fasts and works and expect God to act as we wish, as did the monks of antiquity.[9] Instead of trusting in the Lord's sovereign will, such fasts can appear as blackmail and attempts to manipulate God's will to align with our own. David fasted while his child was dying so that God might grant him his wish. Yet when his child died, he stopped his fasting and humbly accepted God's answer (2 Sam 12:15-23). The prophet Isaiah addresses the same sort of scenario in chapter 58, admonishing those who were impatient with their God who did not act in accordance with their wishes, even though they were fasting. Instead, "when we fast, God *may* in his love, answer our

---

6. Ibid, 46-47.
7. Wimmer, *Fasting in the New Testament*, 14.
8. AE 28:14-15.
9. AE 20:262.

petition"[10] according to our hopes. At the same time, one should perhaps seek to complete a petitionary fast even if that prayer is answered during the fast,[11] to avoid our thinking about fasting as a way of getting "something special out of God [which] is devilish"[12] instead of trusting the outcome to the hidden will of our good and holy God. We ought to dissociate ourselves from the "popular evangelical" mindset that treats prayer or fasting like the placing of a coin in a candy machine and then walking away with the prize. Supposed "faith healers" and "name it, claim it" travelling evangelists foster this idea that God is not sovereign, nor is He truly gracious: He performs for you, based on how well you perform for Him.

A "successful outcome" of our fasting can never be attributed to any of *our* deeds. Even the forgiveness of sins is not brought about by *our* act of repentance, though by repentance expressed in fasting we prepare ourselves to receive it. Dr. C.F.W. Walther, one of the founding Lutheran missionaries and pastors of the Lutheran Church in America, in *The Proper Distinction between Law and Gospel* denounces the well-intended yet misdirected claim that asserts that repentance is a condition for forgiveness as semi-Pelagian.[13] Pious works contribute nothing to our salvation. Not repentance, nor even faith, is a self-generated condition for receiving divine mercy, despite appearances. No one would deny that a beggar cannot receive a coin unless his hands are first cupped, yet that beggar certainly would never attribute the successful reception of that gift to the extension of his cupped hands! Yet even the cupping of the hands with a sincere desire that they be filled is an act of God. We must constantly guard ourselves from attributing success to our own endeavours, though the Old Adam, sin and the devil tempt us daily:

> Those who thought their salvation was based on their 'pious' efforts are scolded in Zechariah 7:5; 8:19 in which the prophet rebukes the ungodly prophets who wanted to attribute their deliverance to their own endeavors like their fasts and not the promises of God.[14]

As discussed earlier, Christian fasting is not so much about changing God as it is about changing us. It is a sacramental way of preparing ourselves

---

10. Wimmer, *Fasting in the New Testament*, 9.
11. Ibid.,15.
12. AE 21:160.
13. Walther, *The Proper Distinction Between Law and Gospel*, 6-12.
14. AE 17:158.

for our Lord's sacramental work in us and for us. God permits and even encourages us to come to Him through fasting (including fasting for specific things). The language in Psalm 22:15—"My mouth is dried up like a potsherd, and my tongue sticks to the roof of my mouth; you lay me in the dust of death"—is designed to move God to take pity and heed the desperate cry of the Psalmist, words that foreshadow and echo the thoughts of the Crucified Christ. Like the divine liturgy, such Psalms of lament ought to be memorized: to "pray it" and not just "say it". God doesn't mind a rightly placed passion and zeal in our piety and prayer life. If prayer is the means of vocalizing our plea at the window of our Lord's heavenly home (Luke 18:1-8), fasts are the fist that raps at His door. As is the case with the persistent widow, who typifies the Church on earth in her sojourn, God promises to respond to His praying and fasting people. And He always answers prayer in accordance with what is best for us. When David's request for the life of his son is denied, he ceases to fast in order to begin glorifying God for hearing his prayer and acting according to His divine wisdom and omniscience. In summary, although both prayer and fasting can become selfish endeavors, they can also exhibit holy ways of glorifying God in humility. The selflessness of fasting is most notably expressed in fasting for others.

Petitionary prayer coupled with fasting for the concerns of others is common practice in the Scriptures and tradition. The role of the Christian as intercessor is a recurring theme in the Holy Scriptures' portrayal of God's people. Fasting is our way of interceding on behalf of others. The author of *Lausiac History*, one of the most important documents for describing early monasticism in Egypt, Palladius (363-431), tells how he fasted for a demon-possessed man, who was cured of his ailment by God.[15] God hears the prayer of a righteous man; He *sees* his fast as well.

One of the functions of the Jewish priest was as a public intercessor for the people.[16] It was also common for the priest as mediator to fast for his people. Christians—the communion of saints—as a universal and royal priesthood (1 Peter 2:9) intercede for the world, just as their pastors inter-

---

15. Palladius, *The Lausiac history*, 58.

16. Incidentally, this fact helps us to understand the case of the Pharisee in Luke 18:12, who is often rebuked for being self-righteous because he prayed out loud publicly. Yet this is unfair. It was expected that he stood before God as one whose fasting and prayer bears on his heart the zeal and woe of the people. In this way, the Pharisee *expects* that he *should* be seen before God (Kittel, *The Theological Dictionary of the New Testament*, 931). The problem is that he stands there in his own stead, trusting in his own deeds, instead of God's mercy, in his appeals.

cede for them. Our common mediator, Jesus Christ our great High Priest, has remarkably chosen to use us all in His salutary plans for the salvation of the dying world today, mystically living in us to carry out His intercessory work. In that sense, we are a means of God's grace to the world, instruments of His forgiveness and sacramental work.[17]

In fasting our hearts are recreated into the heart of God as we share His love for other human beings, "fellow workers" with God (1 Cor 3:9). Our physical hunger mirrors our spiritual hunger for the well-being of others. We thirst for our neighbour's salvation, while we ourselves hang on our own crosses, so that they be embraced by the merciful arms of our ever-loving Lord: "Father, forgive them, for they know not what they do" (Luke 23:34). Our fasting is a living cry for the salvation of our neighbour. It is as normal to fast for the *spiritually dead* as it is to fast in mourning for the *physically de*ad.

> Hunger is usually driven away by prayer and the hungry soul fed exclusively by its supplications. But I am of the opinion that after having prayed, Peter hungered not for food but for the salvation of humankind, and that he was not oppressed by dozily fasting but afflicted by the lack of believers. For when the faithless and ungrateful Jewish people did not believe him when he was preaching Christ, Peter experienced a certain kind of hunger in his ministry.[18]

Each Christian shares this hunger. What we *believe* with our minds about God's desire for all to come to Him, is *felt* in the flesh of the Body of Christ,

---

17. The pastor is priest to believers who are priests to the world in both deeds and words and prayer. Liturgy is not simply the work of God's people inside of a sanctuary but the action of the people of God as a priestly community for the good and welfare and salvation of the world (Elliott, *The Christ Life*, 67). Some examples of this kind of intercession in the Old Testament done by both priests and others are as follows: Nehemiah interceded for others by fasting and praying in times of trouble (Neh 1:4); Ezra interceded on behalf of the nation (Ezra 9:5) while he mourned over the faithlessness of the exiles (Ezra 10:6); Daniel demonstrates intercession for his people in the words of his powerful public confession in which he includes himself with the communal sin ["We have been wicked. We have not listened"(Dan 9:5)]; in 1 Samuel 7:5-6, the nation repents and fasts while Samuel intercedes for their sin; in Joel 2:17 the priests are encouraged to weep before the altar as they pray for their people. This weeping/mourning certainly included fasting which demonstrated their sincerity; in Deuteronomy 9 we hear in verse 18 and following how Moses neither "ate bread or drank water" after witnessing the sin of his people in creating the golden calf while he was with the Lord on Mount Sinai, to deflect God's anger from them. The Lord heard Moses' prayer demonstrated in his fast and had mercy.

18. Maximus, *Sermons*, 17-18.

the Church. The heart of our doctrine and mission beats in fasting. The fasting which often preceded adult baptism (in penitent preparation for the sacrament) reminded God's people of this *Missio Dei*:

> We become close to God in fasting and we mediate for the world through our fasts. Elijah [interrupted] an extreme global drought with a shower to moisten the arid dryness of the earth with the bounty of a heavenly rain. We know in fact that this occurred as a figure of ourselves so that we also who are fasting during the course of these 40 days might merit the spiritual rain of baptism, that a heavenly shower from above might pour down upon the arid ground of the *whole world for our brethren, and the inundation of the saving bath might wet the prolonged drought of the Gentiles.*[19](italics mine)

Fasting for others is as important as fasting for ourselves. If fasting helps us to 'mean' our prayer, and if empathizing with the needs and concerns of others is naturally more difficult than 'empathizing' with our own, then fasting can help us to become more compassionate intercessors for others. It helps us share their burdens in a more genuine or sincere manner, humbling us as *our* needs are pushed aside to make way for *their* needs. Accordingly, *their* prayers, not ours, consume our lives for a given period of time; every hunger pain experienced reminding us constantly of *their* needs, moving us to coordinate each prayer with each hunger pang felt, resulting in the invocation of the Lord's name on *their* behalf several times throughout our day.[20] May our eyes be directed to this picture presented by St. Jerome: "If we are to pray always, then let us fast always: when we pray at night let hunger, not indigestion, affect our breathing" [i.e. the breathing of prayer].[21]

Our hunger reminds us that *we are* praying, heightening the awareness of our spiritual essence: *who* we are as Christians (i.e. the Father's children); *what* we do as Christians (talk to the Father). Orthodox archbishop of Ravenna and exemplary pastor, St. John Chrysologus (406-450) similarly encourages us to fast "that your soul may be a pure offering, a holy sacrifice, a *living victim*, remaining your own and at the same time

---

19. Maximus, *Sermons*, 85-86.

20. Such as through the sending of "arrow prayers" which are fast, short, unprepared, spontaneous cries to the Lord.

21. Jerome, *Letters*, 148.

made over to God".[22](italics mine) We are living victims, incarnations of our living Lord in the suffering flesh of fasting. Just as Anna the Prophetess is characterized by her fasting, we too are characterized by our self-giving. Just as the Blessed Virgin Mary is identified by her suffering tears of sorrow, we too are identified by our love, concern and grief for others. The Church is necessarily a suffering body since, as Spanish mystic St. Teresa of Avila (1515-1582) once spoke, "where love increases so does suffering".

Since sorrow over sin does not always come naturally, such as when we ought to feel deeper contrition for the sin that our prayer requests do not take a higher priority in our lives, the Holy Spirit seeks to train us by self-discipline. Often athletes are not "in the mood" to work-out at the gym. But abiding by a faithful routine helps them maintain their physical endurance. However, even when athletes get lazy, they do not simply stop *being* athletes. Due to the mystical union that we have in Christ who intercedes for the world always, Christians pray constantly for others (Eph 6:18). Yet that promise does not excuse our proactivity in sticking to a routine, even though our neglect does not change our status as children of God and spiritual athletes. And if we find it difficult to pray for the needs of our friends, we will definitely find it more difficult to pray for the needs of our enemies. Yet God asks us to do that too. But when you start, you may find it easier than you thought. After all, Jesus prays through you and so it's hard not to love those for whom you pray—and those for whom you fast. Fasting humbles us and helps us to pray, helps us to empathize, especially with those we happen to despise. So Jesus says, "fast for those who persecute you" (Matt 5:44, 46 f), as was the case with David. In Psalm 35 we hear about how David fasted for his persecutors who mocked him. One wonders how church life might improve if pastors and the faithful were to fast for their 'enemies' before an annual meeting or before a difficult visit to a delinquent member: to see these people through the eyes of not the Lord of glory, the judge, but through the eyes of the suffering, persecuted Christ. One cannot help but wonder how our lives might change if we were to view our enemies through a looking glass from below instead of from above, using our lips to edify and not to curse, saving our words for generous prayers instead of vain accusations. Fasting changes the way that we see other people, and, consequently, how we treat them. Appropriately, Luther suggests that fasting has two primary purposes: "chastising self and serving others . . . The works which come after faith should have [this] sole purpose

---

22. Chrysologus, *Sermons*, 93.

and intention".[23] The two objectives are not mutually exclusive. Many monks of the Middle Ages seemed to believe the contrary, since the value they placed on solitude had very little connection with serving their neighbours outside of praying for them:

> Following the example of Anna the widow in Luke 2:37, in the twelfth century the new monastic orders reaffirmed the ancient tradition of hermit life as a valid expression of spirituality. This widespread movement was characterized by the desire for a simple, solitary life without many of the structures of established monastic houses and their involvement with society. Poverty, solitude, silence, fasting, manual work delineated these new ventures . . . This movement took two forms: there were many hermits, living alone in individual solitude; there were secondly groups of monks living together in corporate solitude.[24]

Though these monks thought that they were serving God by mediating for others *exclusively* in their solitude, both these groups failed to recognize one critical thing: the faster acts as a mediator through prayer yet coupled with deeds. It is difficult to offer good deeds when there is no one around to receive them. It has been said that because prayer accompanies fasting, it should be distinguished from 'abstinence'.[25] The same can be said about almsgiving, to which we will now turn.

---

23. AE 52:139.
24. Jones, *The Study of Spirituality*, 286.
25. Town, *Fasting for Spiritual Breakthrough*, 174.

5

THE TRIADIC NATURE OF FASTING, PRAYER AND ALMSGIVING

FASTING AND PRAYER ARE soul mates, fused together by repentance and a unified appeal to God's mercy.[1] They work as a team. Fasting changes the faster who then changes the world—not just in a hidden "spiritual" sense, but in concrete ways that help other people. *This* is the sort of fasting God also desires.

Isaiah 58 equates a genuine fast with living lives of love; *being* who we already are: God's ambassadors and His tools on earth. The fasting of the Israelites is severely rebuked through the prophet Isaiah for lacking practical, tangible fruits of mercy. In spite of their fasting, they were a people characterized by fighting and arguments. They acted however they pleased, exploiting each other for self interest. They made no attempts to align the principles of their religious lives, which included public fasts, with their everyday lives. In verses 5-6, the prophet explains the sort of fast that does please God, by sketching a brief picture of a believing community in which the needs of one are supplied by the excesses of others. True fasting is not merely fasting but is fasting coupled with showing mercy to brethren[2] by

---

1. Or both if we seek to "pray without ceasing" (I Thess 5:17) and hence "to fast without ceasing" as the Desert Fathers advised when encouraging priests to never fully fill their stomachs but rather to always remain a little hungry.

2. Delitzsch, *The Prophecies of Isaiah III*, 387.

striving for social justice, sharing with the needy, and practicing good works. While establishing his diaconal orders and schools, Wilhelm Löhe—one of the greatest pioneers of Lutheranism in North America—depicts the work of his "Servants of Mercy", the diaconate, as embodying a spirit of fasting, even though he rarely uses the word.[3] Pious deeds demonstrate the sincerity of pious words appealing to the Lord's promise to answer their prayers favourably [see Appendix 1](Zech 7: 9-10; Jas 1:27). True fasting is governed by a heart-felt thought process that acknowledges our total temporal incompleteness, and affirms our individual and communal yearning for the eventual and eternal peace and rest of the new heaven and the new earth, while seeking to season the human journey with hope and promise along the way:

> To be a Christian coincides with being hungry and thirsty, that is an incomplete being, a being in the making, in *statu viae* until the final banquet is held, in *status belli* until resurrection, hungry and thirsty for justice. If we are not in a position to testify to this prophetic outlook, what will be left is a task for dieticians and cooks. If that is all we want, let us indeed leave it to them.[4]

The *true* fast involves a new attitude, seeking opportunities to help our neighbours, and actively tearing down the obstacles which prevent the Holy Spirit from more fully exhibiting the heart of God in our lives. In the sanctified life, striving to love God with our whole heart moves us to see His face in other people. True fasting is then less about self-denial and more about loving sacrifice through self-humbling. Isaiah suggests that if the Israelites seek mercy from God, they should first *show* mercy to others.[5] True fasting is not a material achievement performed for one's own advantage as the prophet Jeremiah underscores in his protest against the "sham holiness" of external observance (Jer 14:12), but true fasting is rather the "bowing of the soul" (Isa 58:5) in moral action.[6] The same message breaks forth from the lips of the prophet Zechariah in 7:1-10 where the people fasted but showed no compassion, mercy or justice to one another. They gave up food but withheld kindness. The oppression of the helpless continued.

---

3. See Willhelm Löhe, *On Mercy: Six Chapters for Everyone, the Seventh for the Servants of Mercy.*
4. Papathanassiou, *Christian Fasting in Postmodern Society*, 268.
5. Leupold, *Exposition of Isaiah II*, 287.
6. Kittel, *The Theological Dictionary of the New Testament*, 928.

These Biblical passages may have been the background for what Christ says in Matthew 5-6 where He treats praying, fasting, and serving the neighbour in the same one breath. These three stand naturally in a triadic relationship. We observe this threefold image in the Church Fathers as well. Peter Chrysologus' sermon during the Lenten season entitled, "prayer knocks; fasting obtains; mercy receives", eloquently articulates the intimate relationship between fasting, prayer and almsgiving and is worth citing at length:

> There are three things, my brethren, which cause faith to stand firm, devotion to remain constant, and virtue to endure. They are prayer, fasting and mercy. Prayer knocks at the door, fasting obtains, mercy receives. Prayer, mercy and fasting: these three are one, and they give life to each other.
>
> Fasting is the soul of prayer, mercy is the lifeblood of fasting. Let no one try to separate them; they cannot be separated. If you have only one of them or not all together, you have nothing. So, if you pray, fast; if you fast, show mercy; if you want your petition to be heard, hear the petitions of others. If you do not close your ear to others you open God's ear to yourself.
>
> When you fast, see the fasting of others. If you want God to know that you are hungry, know that another is hungry. If you hope for mercy, show mercy. If you look for kindness, show kindness. if you want to receive, give. If you ask for your selves what you deny to others, your asking is a mockery.
>
> Let this be the pattern for all men when they practice mercy: show mercy to others in the same way, with the same generosity, with the same promptness as you want others to show mercy to you.
>
> Therefore, let prayer, mercy and fasting be one single plea to God on our behalf, one speech in our defence, a threefold united prayer in our favor.
>
> Let us use fasting to make up for what we have lost by despising others. Let us offer our souls in sacrifice by means of fasting.[7]

7. The rest is worth citing as well:
> Offer your souls to God, make him an oblation of your fasting, so that your soul may be a pure offering, a holy sacrifice, a living victim, remaining your own and at the same time made over to God. Whoever fails to give this to God will not be excused, for if you are to give him your selves you are never without the means of giving.
>
> To make these acceptable, mercy must be added. Fasting bears no fruit unless it is watered by mercy. Fasting dries up when mercy dries up.

THE TRIADIC NATURE OF FASTING, PRAYER AND ALMSGIVING

Self-sacrifice, charity and prayer, are a unity[8] which are encountered and embodied in the one physical fast. The three are so closely tied together that Anna the prophetess (Luke 2:36-38) is held up as a paragon of a piety that expresses itself in fasting and continual prayer, and as a model for the church order of holy widows (Luke 2:27; Acts 6:1; 1 Tim 5:5). Luther describes the relationship similarly, though less poetically, and in more concrete terms in his *Explanation of the Ninety-five Theses*:

> Fasting consists of all chastenings of the flesh apart from the choice of foods or differences in clothes. Prayer includes every pursuit of the soul, in meditation, reading, listening, praying. The giving of alms includes every service toward one's neighbour. Thus by fasting a Christian may service himself, by prayer he may serve God, and by the giving of alms he may serve his neighbour. By means of fasting he may conquer concupiscence of the flesh and live soberly and purely. By means of prayer he may conquer the pride of life and live in a godly manner. By means of giving alms he may conquer concupiscence of the eyes and live righteously in this world.[9]

The triadic relationship is further illuminated in Isaiah 58 in which the prophet encourages those who fast to give up what is fasted to others in need answering *their* prayers (e.g. invite the alien into *your* home, give the hungry *your* food). New Christian traditions of "going without" so that others can "go with" such as families forfeiting their Christmas presents and

---

> Mercy is to fasting as rain is to the earth. However much you may cultivate your heart, clear the soil of your nature, root out vices, sow virtues, if you do not release the springs of mercy, your fasting will bear no fruit.
>
> When you fast, if your mercy is thin your harvest will be thin; when you fast, what you pour out in mercy overflows into your barn. Therefore, do not lose by saving, but gather in scattering. Give to the poor, and you give to yourself. You will not be allowed to keep what you have refused to give others (Chrysologus, *Sermons*, 90-92).

8. So too, Cornelius was held in high regard for his prayer and almsgiving. The Church has held these three in such intimate communion that some argue that textual traditions quickly supplemented these two acts of piety with reference to a third, fasting. In the same way the allusion to prayer in 1 Corinthians 7:5 attracted the textual addition of the notion of fasting in some manuscripts (*Codex Sinaiticus, K,L*)(Freedman, *Isaiah II*, 775). Whatever the case may be, both in Scriptures and tradition the three were tightly linked as testified even in the intertestamental literature. Fasting as an act of devotion alongside prayer and almsgiving is recorded in Tobit 12:8 and Judith 4:9.

9. AE 31:86

redirecting the funds saved to the poor are intended to express this idea.[10] Just as the Christian faster prays and by his fasting gives to others what he has denied himself, so, the pious *almsgiver* does his deeds because he fasts. After all, to give something you possess, to someone else, is nothing other than a fast. The prayer who fasts answers the prayer of the faster who prays. We ought not be surprised that our relational and Triune God would have designed such a lovely symbiotic relationship of mutual interdependence. So, too, the praying Christian will dress up his petition in sincerity by fasting, and may result in the giving up his *time*—which he would have devoted to praying for himself or enjoying another activity—in his praying for someone else. When we fast our time in prayer we practice servanthood towards others—we manifest God's incarnate love towards and among us—, illustrated in these words of St. Peter Chrysologus: "fasting is the soul of prayer and helping the needy is the life blood of fasting".[11] The blood of Christ which pumps through our veins overflows in all forms of Christian charitable service. Patristic literature is bursting with references to charitable fasting such as offering the poor the food spared on Wednesday and Friday fasts, which was the practice of early Christians.[12] Today, our youth groups may encourage an irregular fast as a fundraiser for social causes, or individuals or groups fasting as a means of saving or raising money for the underprivileged. Certainly, the opportunities or occasions are endless, and remain meaningful, not only in their impact on others (regardless of how small) but on their impact on self:

> Come with the strength I lack,
> bring vision clear
> Of human need;
> O give me eyes to see.
> Fulfillment of my life in love outpoured
> My life in You, O Christ, Your love in me.[13]

As Jesus indicates in the washing of His disciples' feet, serving others is the primary way that we serve God (outside of receiving His divine service to

---

10. While being mindful that "the meaning of Christmas" revolves not around our *giving*, but our *getting* of the unique gift of salvation from the incarnate Lord, though generosity in giving is a natural manifestation of our gratitude.
11. Chrysolgus, *Sermons*, 92.
12. Papathanassiou, *Christian Fasting in Postmodern Society*, 267.
13. Frank von Christierson, *Eternal Spirit of the Living Christ*, LSB 769.

us). After all, *God* does not need our good works but our *neighbour* does (Mark 10:45). Jesus as the very embodiment of self-sacrifice best expresses fasting as self-deprivation for the sake of others. His sacrifice on the cross is chiefly to be viewed as a gift to the world. As the medieval symbol of the pelican demonstrates— at a time when it was believed that the mother bird would pierce her own side in order to feed her young starving chicks the food of her flesh—the Son of God empties Himself to fill us up. The crucified One starves Himself to feed the hungry. The crucifix best expresses the uniqueness of Christianity as contradistinctive from all other world religion. The Buddha, fattened with food, sacrifices nothing for the sake of others. He lives only for himself in his aspirations to flee from other cease to exist, regretting the day of his birth. In its purest form, it is the most selfish religion imaginable and, not surprisingly, one of the most popular in North America. In pagan religions, the images are deliberately terrifying, intended to invoke fear, as their disciples serve them in temples, forests and fields, with offerings meant to appease the wrath of the gods or satisfy their personal needs. The absence of images in Islam shows forth a god who is, at best, half-known and at worst, absent. Muslims are rightfully reluctant to describe their Allah in the language of love. Yet the crucifix expresses a *present* God, who has incarnated Himself, not in order to be served by His creation, but to serve them (Mt 20:28). The almighty and self-sufficient Creator becomes weak and helpless to offer Himself for the life of the world. Christ is incarnate love. His death is, indeed, the ultimate fast. And, so, we encounter some early believers confessing that "fasting is better than prayer"[14] to emphasize the centrality of the notion of giving to the Christian Faith. The connection to almsgiving and serving others is so essential that St. Caesarius of Arles (470-543), popular preacher and reformer of Ecclesiastical discipline, taught:

> It is good to fast, brethren, but it is better to give alms. Almsgiving without fasting is enough for a man but fasting without almsgiving does not suffice at all, like a lamp without oil. Just like a lamp which is lit without oil can smoke but cannot give light, so fasting without almsgiving pains the body, to be sure, but does not illuminate the soul with the light of charity. As for our present course of action, brethren, let us in the meantime fast in such a way that we lavish our lunches upon the poor, so that we may not store up in our purses what we intended to eat, but rather in the stomachs of the poor. Truly the hand of the stranger is the treasure of Christ.

14. Towns, *Fasting for Spiritual Breakthrough*, 100.

> Whatever He receives he stores up in heaven so that it will not be lost on earth, because the rewards for a good work are hidden in heaven, even though the food which the poor man receives is consumed. If we strive to lay out our luncheons along the lines of a dinner, with choice delicacies and a multitude of courses, not only are pleasures not taken from our body, but they are even doubled. In this way nothing is gained for the soul, just as nothing is taken from the body.[15]

Fasting then is not practiced for its own sake but for the sake of others. It is not an end to itself but a means, differentiating us from the many self-righteous forms of un-Christian asceticism. Unlike the fasting of the Greeks and Romans, which did not stand in any close relation with ethos and ethics,[16] Christian fasting did. We can say with Jesus in John 4:33, "my food is to do the work of the Father" (John 4:33), while at the same time recognizing our Lord's unique work, as the ultimate faster through His incarnation, temptation and crucifixion, as is prayed in The Litany. In other words, fasting changes the worshipper for social purposes as indicated by Isaiah, Zechariah and even Joel in 2:17 in which 'sparing the people' coincides with fasting. The notion may even be seen symbolically in the Jewish feast of first fruits in which the first cereals and grains were offered to God. This offering was then used to feed others in need (Lev 23:14). Loving others manifests itself in such good works leading some Christians to affirm that when there is a conflict between the fast and the concrete needs of others, the needs of others should be supreme. As fifth century Christian priest, Julianus Pomerius, states,

> It is often beneficial to place hospitality to visitors before fasting or abstinence... We should, however, do our abstaining and fasting in such a manner that we do not put ourselves under the necessity of fasting or abstaining; otherwise, we shall be doing an optional thing under constraint rather than out of piety. If, for instance, in interrupting my fast, I give refreshment to some visitors, I do not break my fast, but I fulfill a duty of charity. Again, if by my abstinence I sadden my spiritual brethren who I know derive enjoyment from my unbending myself, my abstinence should be called not a virtue but a vice because continued abstinence and fasting, unless interrupted when occasion requires, actually makes me vainglorious and saddens my brother, whom charity requires

---

15. Caesarius of Arles, *Fathers of the Church*, 54, 56.
16. Kittel, *The Theological Dictionary of the New Testament*, 927.

> me to serve; and it certainly shows that I have no fraternal charity. For charity alone without abstinence makes any Catholic perfect; and abstinence without the addition of charity either brings about the ruin of all or perishes itself.[17]

By these words Julianus Pomerius reminds us that true piety is reflected in love for others, and that fasting ought to serve *this particular* goal. Fasting always requires us to give up of ourselves (whether food or something else), for the sake of someone else, just as Christ ultimately and perfectly has done for us, in both the incarnation and crucifixion. The notion of self-sacrifice enriches our understanding of the Hebrew word for humbling/afflicting/making oneself poor. God's fast would have His people afflict themselves and deprive themselves, making themselves poor for the sake of the other, as an expression of Christian love. The *Shepherd of Hermas*, the early Christian literary work urging repentance in preparation for the second coming of our Lord, encourages us to "fast and reckon the price of foods which you would have eaten and give it to a widow or an orphan or someone else in need,[18] a dynamic at work in the widow of Zarapeth, who went without food in order to help another (Elijah) (1 Kgs 16 ff). Likewise, St. Augustine states,

> what you have deprived yourself by fasting add to your almsgiving, the time which was formerly taken up in conjugal duties spend in conversation with God; the body which was engaged in carnal love prostrate in earnest prayer; the hands which were entwined in embraces extend in supplication.[19]

So too Luther agrees in *The Blessed Sacrament of the Body of Christ*:

> if men desire to maintain a brotherhood, they should gather a table full of poor people, for the sake of God, the day before they should fast, and on the feast day remain sober, passing the time in prayer and other good works.[20]

These deeds of love will exhibit themselves in a variety of ways in a sincere faster's life, depending on the context. The author of the *Apology of Aristides* more specifically encouraged Christians to seek out the needs of others and then by fasting, gather enough to fulfill those particular needs. By fasting,

---

17. Pomerius, *Ancient Christian Writers*, 98.
18. *The Didache*, 15.
19. Augustine, *Sermons on Liturgical Seasons*, 85.
20. AE 35:68.

some monasteries sent the money saved for overseas missions and thereby, as Greek scholar Origen of Alexandria notes, fasting *actually* nourishes the poor[21] when we give to the hungry what we would have consumed ourselves. In today's context, money saved from purchasing food for oneself could be diverted to humanitarian causes Once again, we are the answer to their prayer for bread. In our culture of excess, how often do we truly experience any deprivation in our stewardship? I certainly do not experience that feeling of "going without" when I put a few dollars in the offering plate. Rarely do my sacrifices affect my spending or eating habits. I may buy a coffee for a homeless person but that doesn't mean that I don't buy one for myself at the same time. But it would be better if it did. In truly denying oneself of something and giving that which is denied to someone else, that gift becomes not only more meaningful to the receiver but also to the giver, because it acts as a 'micro-typology' of God's gift to us in which He denied Himself entirely for us.[22] With a proper understanding of fasting as giving to others by depriving ourselves, Christian mission work becomes more fruitful, not only with augmented funds (we have more to give to others when we do not share the gift with ourselves!), but with that sense of ownership attached to a project in which people actually *feel* their contribution. Although our Christian faith and salvation is certainly not based on subjective emotions, rightly-directed emotions can deepen our belief in those objective truths. When our fasts result in giving from a heart that feels loss, we begin to view others differently, becoming more sensitive to God's presence in those recipients of our sacrifices as "the least of these" (Matt 25:40). Fasting not only changes our economic status (making us more able to give by freeing up things to give), but also changes our attitudes. Fasting shapes our lives and thoughts by heightening our awareness of the poverty of others, both physically and spiritually, instilling in us a more generous spirit. As one Jewish writer comments,

> When we consciously experience hunger, we are more likely to consider the millions who need no [Fast day] in order to suffer hunger. For some, most days are days without food enough for themselves and their children.[23]

---

21. Wimmer, *Fasting in the New Testament*, 52.

22. Some families choose to use the money that they would have normally spent on Christmas presents for each other to buy Christmas presents for a less fortunate family in their congregation.

23. Knobel, *Jewish Fasts: Gates of the Seasons*, 50.

THE TRIADIC NATURE OF FASTING, PRAYER AND ALMSGIVING

Our 'voluntary' fasting allows us to better relate with the needs of others and become attentive of their 'involuntary fasting' which is often a starvation that may take some atypical and diverse forms.[24] Such cognizance frees us from over-concentrating on ourselves and allowing us to respond more selflessly to the needs of others.[25]

This denial of self has an added bonus as it is indeed freeing in and of itself. The Augustinian maxim, 'to diminish one's need rather than to increase one's possession'[26] teaches us that happiness does not consist in possessing and consuming much, but in having few needs and satisfying them at small expense.[27] Yet the effects of fasting impact us on a more profound level, a teaching which embodies the essence of the sacraments. The Sacraments involve a conscious sensitivity to and awareness of all that the Divine Spirit is now doing in the present to save, reconcile, and make His people alive and whole.[28] Fasting confesses our role in this process by joining us to the sufferings *in* the world, in order to bring healing *to* the world, *through* Christ:

> The healthy man does not know what the sick man feels. The man who is well fed does not know what the hungry man feels. The sick man more readily feels with the sick and the hungry with the hungry. For just as pure truth is seen only with a pure heart, so he who is wretched at heart feels more truly with the wretchedness of his brother.[29]

We suffer with the hungry man and all those who suffer and are thereby transformed back into the likeness of Christ, mystically becoming the *man* Christ was. Thomas of Celano, the first biographer of St. Francis of Assisi, spoke of fasting in terms of sharing in "the humility of the incarnation" of Christ, a bearing on the body of the marks (i.e. *stigmata*) of Jesus (Gal 6:17).[30] Christians are known by these marks. Their love, their sufferings, their fasts are characteristics of Christian ownership by God. They are the visible and invisible signs of Christ's sacramental presence within and

---

24. Wimmer, *Fasting in the New Testament*, 118.

25. Ibid., 117.

26. Adalbert de Vogüé, *The Rule of Saint Benedict: Doctrinal and Spiritual Commentary*, 236.

27. Ibid., 233.

28. Elliott, *The Christ Life*, 35.

29. Bernard, *Selected Works*, 106.

30. Pelikan, *The Illustrated Jesus Through the Centuries*, 145.

amongst believers. The broken Body of Christ is encountered in the broken body of the faster and His fasting people. Fasting's sacramental character is revealed in this configuration. It is in this light that Christian fathers of the Church such as St. Francis understood fasting as a conformity to Christ in His crucifixion.

> A direct corollary of identifying the sufferings of his body with the sufferings of Christ was a new and deeper awareness of the humanity of Christ, as disclosed in his nativity and sufferings.[31]

When those "who radically share the little they have in order to support others who may be even worse off"[32] we have a beautiful expression of concrete *material* solidary of the members of the Body of Christ. So too, the Desert Fathers would claim that the primary function of fasting is less individualistic as it is communitarian: not so much deepening our reliance upon the mercies of God, but, rather, helping us to love our brothers and sisters with more intensity—alleviating the temptation towards making fasting an egocentric act of highly individualized personal piety. Fasting is not an end in itself.[33] Rather, it brings humility in allowing us to see others as greater than ourselves.[34] The Christian ascetic—in the best sense of that phrase—who looks in the mirror does not see a pretty sight, but is rather confronted with the face of a dirty, undernourished, poor, scummy and dependent sinner. It is in this state that one can honestly say along with Desert Father Abbot Allois, "I alone and God are in this world".[35] The Christian strives to see himself as the only sinner, surrounded by a company of saints upon whom the holy image of God has been impressed, while mindful that other Christian saints are considering him, and their brothers, in the exact same way. After all, the innocent Christ surely considered Himself as the only sinner who alone could and did carry the massive load of our sin and permanently nailed it to the cross while we, to whom those filthy loads rightfully belong, are emptied, cleaned and freed. We are Christ's Body, yet not exclusively. An ascetic approach to others shapes the way we see them as the Body of Christ (or at least potentially so) and may perhaps bring

---

31. Ibid.,150.
32. Witetschek, *Going Hungry for a Purpose*, 385.
33. Waddell, *The Desert Fathers*, 100.
34. Ibid, 120.
35. Waddell, *The Desert Fathers*, 13.

them to the point where they will say of us what they said of abbot Macarius the elder,

> that even as God doth protect all the world, and beareth the sins of men, so was he to the brethren as it might be an earthly God, for he covered up their faults, and what things he saw or heard, it was as though he saw not and heard not.[36] One can learn a lot from the words of Abbot Daniel: "the body withers; the soul flourishes".[37]

God uses our fasts to heal this broken world as fasting transforms our communities socially, physically and spiritually. But that wider transformation begins with the narrow transformation of *my* spirit, by the hand of our transfiguring God who brings those changes in me, sacramentally. Fasting assists in making us sacramental people in a non-sacramental world which hungers for the proclamation of the Gospel. Fasting proclaims this message to the world . . . visibly.

---

36. Ibid., 155.
37. Ibid., 100.

6

THE EVANGELICAL MESSAGE OF FASTING

As the body of Christ the Church shares in the sacramental role of her lordly Head. As salt and light and children of peace, she manifests in and to the world the flavor, radiance and unity of life revealed by her exalted Lord[1] ... *Sacramental living is the Church in mission.* It is not simply missionaries talking or speaking good news to man, but being God's mission to the world, being and effecting the good news, being the sacramental bearer and celebrant of God's glorious presence in the world.[2]

FASTING CHANGES THIS TEMPORAL world in concrete ways, such as freeing more financial resources to help others in need. Not only does it help to change economic situations, it helps to change souls. We are instruments of God in the conversion of others who consume our Gospel words by their ears, and taste their fruits by our deeds. This is not just the case for Christians as individuals, but also as a community of believers. The Church as a body communicates theology in corporate words and corporate deeds. Earlier we discussed numerous examples of corporate fasting in the Scriptures. As was the case with Ezra, a national concern requires a national fast. This should not surprise us when considering the corporate nature of the body of believers, a Christian ethos and way of thinking that has

1. Elliott, *The Christ Life*, 73.
2. Ibid.

unfortunately been lost in hyper-individualistic Western society. Yet fasting joins us to the larger community of hurting and hungry people, offering us a precious and rare opportunity to respond to their needs in both empathy and sympathy. For,

> in fasting, there is the opportunity to reflect upon the nature of suffering as it begins with, but ultimately exceeds, the experience of corporeal suffering. Here Christians encounter an opportunity to consider not only the suffering specific to rational beings, as it encompasses the entirety of the being, both soul and body, but also how it is that God, although incorporeal and thus impassible, can himself be said to suffer.[3]

We join the suffering of others and meet them in their desert as equals, in order to lead them to an oasis from which springs forth living water unto eternity (John 4:10). Thus, not only does fasting teach the fasters something profound about their faith, a subject which will be discussed later, it also sends a vital message to those outside of the believing community. We have already established how charity is intrinsically connected to fasting. The ways and reasons for our fasts demonstrates to the pagan and heathen the wonderfully and radically difference between our God and theirs. Fasting announces a *doctrinal message*, causing the heathen to reconsider his humanistic worldview. It tells of God's severe judgement upon sin, and His eagerness for showing mercy. Daniel would not eat foods dedicated to idols primarily in honour of God, but also as a public confession of faith concerning the identity of the only true and living God. Likewise, St. Paul teaches us to abstain from foods (e.g. food dedicated to idols), not for our own sake, but for the sake of others in order to prevent them from either falling away or to present a clear witness to the unbeliever (Rom 14:20-21; 1 Cor 8:13). Abstaining from foods reminds other believers who they are, and teaches unbelievers *who they too can become*. Fasting in Judea-Christian tradition functioned as a proclamation about the living God. It still does today. Yet the present-day religious Jews, unfortunately, proclaim a different message today since they have rejected the Messianic promises fulfilled in Christ. At the same time, numerous Jewish fasts—as "Christian" fasts, *pre the incarnation of the Second Person of the Holy Trinity*—while existing in the pre-Christian epoch exhibited a joyful undertone in so far as they point forward to the coming of our Messiah. For instance in Yom Kippur a glimpse of the

---

3. Loughlin, *Thomas Aquinas and the importance of fasting to the Christian life*, 357.

forthcoming Gospel and resurrection joy is spotted in that believers are encouraged to socialize with strangers and discouraged from wearing black in spite of the solemnities of the event.[4] Even the fast on the day of the assassination of Geddaliah which is "to teach you that the death of righteous people is as the burning of the House of the Lord",[5] foreshadowed the event of the cross—building up hope in the Resurrection. Because of Christ, even the mournful and repentant fasts of Christians always contain hints of happiness (see Appendix II) and are thankful expressions of joy,[6] methods of praise, and testimonies to the world. Although we weep that Christ died; we rejoice that Christ rose. "With reason do we mourn if we burn with desire for Him".[7] "Through fasting, Christians seal their minds and hearts to what must be done and declare in this very discipline a hope in that which lies beyond the everyday natural desires of this world".[8] Although we are sad that we live in the 'not yet'; we are happy that we live in the 'already'. The sacraments have often been described as "'actions of celebration': in the midst of death it celebrates life".[9] Fasts belonging to this celebrative event are properly understood as 'sacramental actions' since they eschatologically involve a "commemoration, demonstration, and anticipation"[10] of the work of Christ. After all, "fasting signifies anticipation [and] waiting, whereas a feast reflects fulfillment; the Christian *eschaton* or arrival of the kingdom in its glory and joy."[11] The visual expression in some traditions of women wearing Easter bonnets to church on Easter Sunday in contrast with the black "sackcloth" of Lent, drives this point home visually.

> In this perspective, fasting becomes "an icon of the future life" insofar as it is an act that introduces into everyday life a foretaste of the eschatological freedom from necessity. In bold outline, here

---

4. Block, *The Biblical and Historical background of Jewish Customs and Ceremonies*, 170. Abraham Block records an entire listing of Jewish fast days and how these periods of fasting point to, or are typological of, Christ Jesus.

5. Ibid., 347.

6. AE 21:155.

7. Augustine, *Sermons on Liturgical Seasons*, 100.

8. Loughlin, *Thomas Aquinas and the importance of fasting to the Christian life*, 359.

9. Elliott, *The Christ Life*, 40.

10. Ibid., 35.

11. Larin, *Feasting and Fasting According to the Byzantine Typikon*, 142.

lie the criteria of Christian fasting: understanding the world as creation, the expectation of the eschaton, and love in practice.[12]

This evangelical message of hope in our dark and spiritually constricting world consumed early Christian thought. In order to teach the unbeliever that Christianity was the fulfillment of Judaism, and hence a superior religion,[13] the early Church taught that Christians should fast Wednesdays and Fridays and not Mondays and Thursdays so that they would avoid being confused with the Jews and Hypocrites.[14] The reason being: Jews fasted on Monday and Thursday since Moses received the Law on a Thursday and came down on a Monday.[15] In contrast to the remembrance of the Law, Christians fasted in remembrance of the Gospel, the fulfillment and liberation from the Law. As recorded in the Didache 8:1, Christians were to fast on Wednesdays, the day in Holy Week that the plot against Jesus began to be carried out (or "spy Wednesday" when the Jews held a council to betray our Lord), and Friday, the day our Lord was betrayed and crucified.[16] Fish on Fridays is a cultural reminder of this Friday fasting . . . although, I suppose "meat on Fridays" may be a more appropriate alternative for seafood lovers. Incidentally, the preference for fish seems to have been caused by the belief that the ground was cursed after the Fall from Eden but the water, and all the fruits thereof, were, evidently, unaffected. This selective and arbitrary neo-Pelagian view between "clean" and "unclean" material, resulted in an

---

12. Papathanassiou, *Christian Fasting in Postmodern Society*, 256.

13. Many non-Christians, especially the Jews, held fasting in high regard as a form of religious piety. The continuance of Christians in these fasts gave greater credibility to their words. John the Baptizer was respected as a prophet because of his piety, as fasting for the Jews was a sign of holiness (Matt 11:18; Lk 7:33) and voluntary fasting had widespread approval as a mark of religious devotion (Freedman, *Isaiah II*, 776). Up until the New Testament fasting came to occupy so high a place in the practice and estimation of Judaism, that for the Gentiles it became one of the marks of the Jew (Kittel, *The Theological Dictionary of the New Testament*, 929). The *Testaments of Twelve Patriarchs* makes frequent reference to fasting as a hallmark of piety. The Essenes were regular fasters as well (Freedman, *Isaiah II*, 776). Although fasting was not theologically mandatory for the Christian, it definitely helped in the Christians' witness to the Jews, strengthening their polemic. Even Luther comments that fasting is good so that "no one would have the right to accuse us of despising and completely rejecting the practice of fasting" (AE 21:160).

14. *The Didache*, 19.

15. Block, *The Biblical and Historical background of Jewish Customs and Ceremonies*, 350.

16. Ibid., 26.

elaborate system of legalistic, and even Levitical, distinctions between and prohibition of foods in the Medieval Church, and was the source of attack by the greater defender of the Reformation, Martin Chemnitz.[17] Chemnitz argued that Essene influences and pagan philosophies and superstitions had crept into church piety and corrupted the practice of fasting.[18] In short, vegetarians were not off the hook! Yet, at the same time, due to the atoning work of Christ, all foods are now clean (Mark 7:19: Acts 10:15). The way that Christians fast sends a message, for the better or the worse.

In any case, the Friday fast was practically universal in the Church. In AD 31, Epiphanus, bishop of Salamis, asked, "who does not know that the fast of the fourth and sixth days of the week are observed by Christians throughout the world?"[19] Later, the Franciscans insisted that the Friday fast was the foremost, in order to remind the world of Good Friday.[20] In this way, it was hoped that the unbeliever would see that the Christian is not the Jew of the old covenant but the Jew of the new. So too this evangelical, 'mission minded' reasoning is manifested in other decisions of the Church as well. The Sabbath rest was intentionally moved to Sunday as a public reminder that Christians are no longer under the Law because of Christ, a weekly celebration of the Resurrection on the third day. The weekly fasts demonstrate both Law and Gospel at work: we are exposed in our sin by the heavy demands of God to be perfect in loving Him and others, but we have hope in a Saviour who has achieved for us all that our fasting could never achieve for itself. Indeed, He is Himself, by His atoning sacrifice, the answer and end to all of our fasting. The Christian reveals, not only his own particular sins, but all of humankind's global sin in all its monstrosities through the midweek fast. He acts as a microcosm of humanity as if he alone is the sinner in the sackcloth and ashes of his repentance, and the hunger and thirst of his heart. Then, the Christian celebrates God's goodness in the universal cleansing of these sins, through the Sunday feast; that is, the feast of thanksgiving when the Lord feeds His people with His crucified flesh and blood. Thus, the Eucharistic service always ends the fast.[21] In

---

17. For a thorough discussion as to why these "papalistic" distinctions are arbitrary, see "Concerning the Manner or Way with Food During Fasting, and of the Choice, the Distinction, or the Prohibition of Foods" in Chemnitz, *Examination of the Council of Trent IV*, 275-285.

18. Chemnitz, *Examination of the Council of Trent IV*, 285, 337-341.

19. Towns, *Fasting for Spiritual Breakthrough*, 1996.

20. Sullivan, *Fast and Abstinence in the First order of St. Francis*, 27.

21. Hunter, *Preaching in the Patristic Age*, 40.

fact, in an effort to preserve joyfulness on the eighth day, the day of our Lord's resurrection and sacramental feast, many early Christians even forbade fasting on Sundays.[22] In today's world, unless we live in an orthodox Jewish neighbourhood, separating ourselves visually from the Jews is probably less relevant than distinguishing ourselves from the neo-pagan world. It is tragically unfortunate that more people, for whom God has so generously given His life and wishes to share in the joy of that message, are either disinterested, or unaware, of what is going on for them within the churches in their neighbourhoods. Fasting reminds us, and them, that our spiritual hunger is only satisfied in Jesus Christ, the only true nourishment. Are we courageous enough to tell them? Our fasting provides us with a unique opportunity to begin such a dialogue.

Fasting then as a public confession displays our gratitude and humility before God (i.e. publicly expressing our dependence and His omnipotence),[23] but more importantly, it is an acknowledgement of our mortality: the absence of food is death, 'the indefinite fast', and is thus an expression of our beliefs in a future life.[24] After all, every corpse fasts—naturally—and yet, in Christ, buried and resurrected, each baptized and believing Christian has a place in His heavenly Kingdom (Gal 3:27).

Fasting is a prayer of confidence in God's provisions; He supplies for all of our needs in the present and hereafter. The weakness of hunger points towards death (both physical and spiritual) and indicates human helplessness outside of life with Christ.[25] On the one hand "my own anguish calls forth the anguish of others, it reminds them of their own emptiness and isolation".[26] On the other hand, the fasting and suffering Christian is a living witness to our fasting and suffering Lord, a physical embodiment of the truth that though we are dead and helpless, yet we possess a hidden hope in Christ our help and life.

> Fasting and its accompanying rites of weeping, rending clothes, donning sackcloth, and applying ashes function as a physical manifestation and communicative expression of anguish and affliction:

---

22. Brattston, *Fasting in the Earliest Church*, 241, 245.
23. Wimmer, *Fasting in the New Testament*, 118.
24. Ibid.
25. Ibid., 119.
26. Nouen, *Heart Speaks to Heart*, 21.

"see how awful is my state". Such extreme expression is employed in mourning the dead.[27]

Thus, fasting rejects any manifestations of stoicism that we find in modern culture and society. Even though the Stoics fasted, it was for "inner peace by self control, increasing the power of reason" which is far removed from the humility and penance and supplication connected to the Christian fast,[28] whose help comes not from inside himself but from outside and from above. Moreover, fasting flies in the face of popular neo-gnostic tendencies today—ones that despise the body while exalting the soul—since it acknowledges the unity of body and soul/mind in the one person and the necessity and goodness of the material world. God provides for both spiritual and bodily needs. Flesh and spirit, consistent with the Scriptural presupposition, are ontologically inseparable.[29] In his *Letters* St. Paulinus of Nola (355-431) writes:

> Paul says that each one should know how to possess his vessel in honour that he may present his body as a living sacrifice pleasing to God, not filling the flesh because when the body is satiated it kills the sobriety of the soul and is hostile to chastity (I Thess 4:4; Rom 21:1).[30]

The Gnostics either cared too little about the body or too much,[31] depending upon how each sect understood its inferior relationship to the spirit (i.e. whether to have nothing to do with it as inferior matter, or whether to treat it indifferently, by indulgence and abuse, as inferior matter). Christians honour the body as a good gift of God, care for it as God's spiritual temple on earth. After all, the body will be resurrected on the final day. Moreover, God assumed our flesh through the Blessed Virgin Mary and remains forever incarnate for us, exemplifying the high value He places on His redeemed creation. For this reason, cremation has never been a Christian tradition as its practice historically is undergirded by a theology that seeks

---

27. Lambert, *Fasting as Penitential Rite*, 479.

28. Wimmer, *Fasting in the New Testament*, 24.

29. Although St. Paul's letters occasionally make morally superlative distinctions between the body/flesh and soul/mind in order to demonstrate the work of the Holy Spirit in contrast with the work of the flesh, Western Philosophical categories that radically disconnect the two are foreign to Scripture.

30. Paulinus, *Letters*, 286.

31. "The heretics (Manicheans) detest the flesh" and think that they "can better themselves and become perfect by abstinence" (Pomerius, *Ancient Christian Writers*, 98).

to free the soul eternally from the "cage" of the body. But the Christian cares little for the body in itself due to its sinful state but honours it for the sake of its unity with the flesh of Christ. This confession of the goodness of the body accounts for many Christian practices, such as anointing with oil (James 5:14-15), applying medicine, so to speak, in the name of Lord. This confession reaches its peak in the sacraments, where God unites Himself with the material world.

> The reverence for life, the care for the body, the whole medical mission of the church—all is a natural result of salvation through the flesh and Resurrection of the flesh.[32]

From bodily experience we learn spiritual things. The tacit assumption that asceticism like fasting, by its very nature, always entails a pessimistic worldview and a body-soul dualism, is without basis.[33] Instead the practice presents a balanced/realistic worldview, which includes a "pessimistic" side. It reveals man for what he is: a needy sinner before God *qua* body and soul. It serves as a picture of our place within the divine hierarchy [and yet the King descends to us as one who serves! (Luke 22:27)]. Do penitential poses, such as, genuflecting and bowing in the presence of royalty indicate a demeaning view of one's own self? It is recognition that you are not in the presence of equals, and, yes, that you are in a sense "inferior". And how much greater does the logic apply when you find yourself in the presence of the King of kings and Lord of lords? In fact, a full prostration, touching the forehead to the ground, is a physical expression both of repentance and of a determination to rise again from sin, according to St. Basil.[34] The Lenten fast was so important to the early Christians, even to the point of making it mandatory for all believers,[35] because it is a powerful public proclamation and communal pronouncement of the Law. It is, in fact, a visual manifestation of Christian doctrine. As we have discussed in a previous chapter, although we are not all monks, we are all, in a sense, *ascetics*: "*Ascesis* is not an exceptional task pertaining to a special group within the Church, but it coincides with Church membership. Every Christian is an ascetic"[36] as we live out what it means to be a new creation in Christ and members of

---

32. Elliott, *The Christ Life*, 29.
33. Freedman, *Isaiah II*, 775.
34. Larin, *Feasting and Fasting According to the Byzantine Typikon*, 145.
35. Augustine, *Sermons on Liturgical Seasons*, 99-100.
36. Papathanassiou, *Christian Fasting in Postmodern Society*, 258.

His Body with the mandate to influence the world for the better. After all, the Lord would have killed us immediately after our Baptism, to spare us from the theoretical possibility of losing our saving faith, if He didn't have a plan for us in reshaping the fallen world around us. Some Christians have tragically overemphasized the importance of social action in its relationship to eternal salvation, but that abuse does not discredit its important use for the Kingdom of God. Because of the multiplicity of meanings implicit to food consumption in our society, fasting sends a powerful message:

> In the Christian perspective, both feasting and fasting have a strong communal dimension; every attitude toward food is an act of sharing. Besides, in a world which tends to multiply meanings and symbolism, the Church ought to welcome this trend as a quest for truth and respond to it with her own belief that the truth of the world is a Person who lies beyond the constituent parts of the world and beyond decay, and that it is precisely because of this otherness that He can give the world what its constituent parts cannot afford—life abundant.[37]

The modern hunger strike, intended to attract attention to a practice deemed unfair or unbearable[38]—a "protest rather than penitence"[39]—is a desperate enactment of a plea in the hope and certainty of being remembered by the governing authority, and resembles the Biblical lament:

> Fasting is an extreme stark expression of one's affliction that tends towards overstatement or exaggeration of the desperation of the situation in order to arouse attention and elicit sympathy. The refusal to eat, like the lamenter's refusal to fall silent, is in many ways the last recourse of protest when one feels powerless to change the course of events.[40]

Appealing to the compassion of political leaders—who, at the very least, have an invested electoral interest in appearing somewhat sympathetic—a hunger strike can be compared to the "timeout" in the child's game of tag: an unwritten rule superseding all other rules; to ignore it is to disrespect all other players as it appeals to an inviolable communal value. Though bearing no legal weight, it has a powerful influence, nevertheless. Such fasting is a means of awakening our society to issues that were previously

---

37. Ibid., 256.
38. Lambert, *Fasting as a Penitential Rite*, 482.
39. Lambert, *Fasting as a Penitential Rite*, 482.
40. Ibid.

neglected or considered unimportant, and forcing us to respond. When King David cuts himself off from his normal social networks and rejects all personal comforts by his fast, he forces his friends and subjects, who are embarrassed by his behaviour, to react. The self-righteous shake their heads in disappointment, disgusted by the way fasting alters physical appearances (Ps 69:11-12). These revilers become unwillingly involved in the event, whether they like it or not. So, too, Esther becomes greatly agitated when she discovers Mordecai fasting and wearing sackcloth because of the potential societal effect of his behaviour (Esther 4:4). Society, "which as to maintain its own integrity, has a stake in preventing individuals from slipping into the stark and horrid".[41] The secular world, presuming they understand the meaning of ashes spread upon Christian foreheads, ought to take deep offense, since it recalls the pathetic condition of *their* spiritual state along with our own. Behind the white picket fences of "First World" affluence and materialism hide condemned homes infested by the pests of sin and the irreversible mould of despair. Who wants to think about himself as greedy and selfish, or a spiritual failure; that a clean-cut decent person could actually reside under the judgement of God? It is a slap to the facade of our pride, independence, self sufficiency and all positivistic values of social evolution and human progress. Fasting provides a "mirror through which the horror and starkness of the individual's assumed stance can be viewed."[42] Instead, "God raises the poor from the dust and lifts up the needy from the dunghill." (Ps 113:7)

Like us today, the Christian Fathers of the past wanted to affect the world by their fasting out of a genuine zeal for societal improvement and the conversion of others. During times of public manifestations of intolerable immorality,

> throughout all the churches a public fast was imposed so that those miserable men might realize they had committed such a great evil that it was necessary for all the churches to fast on account of their sins. For this reason, dearest brethren, let us fast on these days, and with a true and perfect charity let us grieve over the foolishness of miserable men, so that they may understand their wickedness as they see a public fast being observed for them. For we should not despair that through your prayer and abstinence God may correct them, for with ineffable goodness He promised this through His apostle when he said, "the person who brings a sinner back from

---

41. Ibid., 486.
42. Ibid., 488.

his way will save his soul from death and cancel a multitude of sins (James 5:20).[43]

Fasting is a beautiful expression of love for the other. Next to death, no single "religious" deed measures up to the message it sends to the world: our ugliness in self, and our beauty in Christ. Obviously, it is not easy to fast publicly. The world thinks it is foolish. Ashes on the foreheads of the fasting faithful Body on the day of Ash Wednesday—commencing the holy season of Lent—a sign of death and mourning, is at best the subject of curiosity, and at worst, an object of ridicule. Who would choose to appear in public with a dirty face? Fasting is, after all, a radical and violent rejection of secular values and modern culture: "Christians are called to reject naturalism" and form a way of life that flows against the secular tides.[44] So in spite of a foolish appearance, or perhaps we could say *because* of a foolish appearance, it arouses consciences in the same way that a hunger strike forces a response from each and every observer; some to anger, others to laughter, and still others to conversion. In Psalm 69:10 we hear how David humbled his soul for his enemies but was insulted over it. David became so weak by fasting that others mocked him (Ps 109:24). He foreshowed our Lord Jesus Christ. For the cries of the Psalmist were also the cries of the man Jesus fasting in the desert and fasting on the cross, hanging empty and hungry and helpless. Likewise, the Christian is always, in some manner or other, persecuted for the Faith; a universal truth expressed in the particularity of fasting. And yet, it is never undergone in vain. The word or work of one person goes a long way. The entire nation of Nineveh was converted to the true Faith through the warnings of the single prophet Jonah—the catalyst to their fasting and repentance—in spite of his reluctance and lack of enthusiasm for the cause.

---

43. Caesarius of Arles, *Sermons*, 29.
44. Papathanassiou, *Christian Fasting in Postmodern Society*, 256.

7

FASTING AS CATECHESIS

FASTING DOESN'T JUST SEND a message to the world but also to us. It is catechetic. As Christians who find ourselves situated in the affluent environment of Western society in contrast with the vast array of war-torn, poverty-stricken nations, fasting teaches us about our global responsibilities.

In view of the economically underdeveloped world, fasting is a 'symbolic sacrifice' that helps us better appreciate the food we have,[1] while also reminding us of our call to help the poor in their spiritual and physical health. Fasting changes our eating habits by making us realize just how little food we actually need in order to live.[2] The lessons learned are likely to carry on well after the fast is complete. Money saved by spending less on food for ourselves and given to the hungry through mission budgets, much like the "30 Hour Famine" which some youth groups undergo, is as didactic as it is helpful.[3]

> While in older society [fasting's] meaning was organized around festivities, today it has acquired a huge number of social connotations as central to almost every aspect of life.[4]

1. Berry, *Fasting Safely*, 1.
2. Ibid., 3.
3. Some church youth groups have banquets of rice and beans to remember the hungry and give the money saved to the poor. In India they take a cup of rice from their food supply (or some other valuable grocery) and resell it for missions.
4. Papathanassiou, *Christian Fasting in Postmodern Society*, 251.

In other words, the symbolic functions of fasting bear greater weight today than in antiquity because of the increasingly complex roles that food plays in our society. Through Christian fasting, we insert a necessary and effective voice into the public discourse as well, avoiding a "heavenly mindedness" that keeps us from being of any "earthly good", in the words of Martin Luther. Public and visible displays of fasting are not intended to "show off" our piety but are repentant statements and humble witnesses to the unbelieving world recalling our communal guilt and responsibilities. Accordingly, most charitable organizations and movements, historically and globally, boast Christian roots. As saints, Christians care for others as much as they do for themselves, which ought to prod the unbeliever to ask the question, "Why?" For those who have "eyes to see and ears to hear" Christian fasting offers an explanation. Christians take the moral and ethical concerns of the secular world seriously, especially in places where they overlap with our own, despite a different place that those values may take in our respective belief systems. For instance,

> [t]hat we as human beings can ruin our own home, that is destroy the ecological balance on the planet, was inconceivable in earlier centuries. Likewise, advanced food technology that seems to defy the flow of the season and the climate, was something unthinkable. They are both new realities, tightly bound to man's relations with food. They both nourish the gigantism of egoism and the self-consciousness of humans as the overlords and proprietors of the world. Thus, insofar as the Church conceives of the world as a gift (not an asset) and understands receiving food as an act of thanksgiving (not as a mechanical procedure), then the issue of fasting cannot be examined separately from the issue of food production and hedonism, which is ready to sacrifice everything for its own satisfaction... For example, what kind of respect toward God's creation does the Christian show when he consumes fish without paying any attention to the problem of overfishing that jeopardizes the very existence of certain species on earth? Is it really a Christian attitude to fasting when we eat kiwi fruit produced in economies based on ruthless child labor or vegetables irrigated with water containing lethal hexavalent chromium? Why doesn't our way of thinking become relevant to the contemporary world, forming new ways of fasting?[5]

---

5. Papathanassiou, *Christian Fasting in Postmodern Society*, 265.

Yet, most importantly, "relevance" concerns questions of eternity over and above temporality. The fact that "man does not live on bread alone" (Matt 4:4) suggests a lesson regarding both body and soul. We need food to survive physically. So, too, we need a different kind of food to survive spiritually. Fasting teaches us about our spiritual hunger being satisfied uniquely in Christ, the Bread from heaven. The lack of food, and even our hunger pains, remind us of our mortality, our bodily dependence on food, which is a type or shadow—in the language of Plato—of the 'real' food, the heavenly food, the flesh of God without which we cannot live both now and forever. Thus, when we pray, "Give us this day our daily bread", we pray for both kinds of food, with the emphasis certainly on the latter, and appropriately prayed prior to the Liturgy of the Holy Sacrament of the Altar. In keeping with the Christian tradition of sharing an *Agape* meal along with the Lord's Supper, Coptic orthodox Christians set aside and apart a portion of their leavened bread to be consecrated for the Holy Eucharist. This bread is then handed out afterwards as breakfast to members and non-communicant visitors alike. With a similar intent, many protestant churches offer potlucks, meals or coffee fellowship after their services. The Church has always concerned Herself with both kinds of bread, for both the body and the soul. Yet the emphasis, naturally, remains upon eternal nourishment. It is marvelous how God exhibits His Gospel message in various ways, drawing on a variety of teaching methods. Throughout life, God teaches us. He draws us ever closer to Him and His Word, through the whole variety of life experiences, some voluntary, and others involuntary, both good and bad. Even through our basic human necessities God teaches us this truth: that we are totally and completely dependent upon the Creator. In the Scriptures we *hear*, and in fasting we *feel*, that the Lamb is indeed the Bread of life. From bodily experience we learn spiritual things, namely that,

> by symbolically denying the most basic biological necessity which humans share with all animals, we focus on that aspect of human nature which we share with God.[6]

We are God's unique redeemed creatures and He wants us to know it, constantly. So much so, that He does not limit Himself only to His Word, but also uses our unique experiences of suffering and joy in His pedagogy. God is, so to speak, "obsessed" with the Gospel, and uses everything and anything to lead us through the path of repentance to the ever-flowing fount of

---

6. Knobel, *Jewish Fasts*, 53.

His all-consuming love. Accordingly, it is the Holy Spirit's desire that every one of our experiences brings us back to our baptismal identity.

The Old Testament Israelites also understood how fasting teaches about the Messiah. Hence Yom Kippur for the Jews was the most important fast of the year, the only prescribed fast[7] as it pointed to the most important event in history, the Day of Atonement, when the Messiah would come and give rest to His people once and for all by atoning for the sins of the world (Lev 23:27). This great news is observed in all the events of the festival: it is a fast of waiting in expectation for God's forgiveness found in Christ, encompassing ten days of repentance, self examination, confession, and self-denial.[8] The Day of Atonement is the only day in which the Holy of Holies is entered, illuminating the event in the temple during the crucifixion of our Lord—the tearing of the curtain which separated common man from our holy God and granting us permanent access. The Day also included a prayer for world peace, achieved exclusively by the risen Christ through His atonement.[9] It is, then, a day of repentance but also of joy, a celebration of the reconciliation of God to man.[10] Fasting on this day, as on any day, connects present events with past ones, joining the individual with the greater Church Body.

> Yom Kippur is a day of concentration on the past so that the future may be better for us . . . Despite its solemnity, Yom Kippur is also a day of joy, when the truly penitent person begins gradually to feel at one with God and humankind. Reconciliation is the goal of the day's prayers and fast. When the final blast of the *Shofar* is heard at the end of the *Ne-ilah*, those who have observed the day with sincerity should feel that they have been inscribed and sealed in the book of life.[11]

In fasting we join ourselves with our brethren of the past, reliving historical events. For the Jews, Purim Day was a re-enactment of the events in which Queen Esther saved her people from the Persian enemy, Haman. By following the fast with a feast, the community remembers the deliverance

---

7. This fast is the most strictly observed (Lev 16:29,31; 23:27,3; Num 29:7). One *Mishnah* asserts that if as much as one drop of saliva is consumed the fast has been broken (Kittel, *The Theological Dictionary of the New Testament*, 8)!

8. Knobel, *Jewish Fasts*, 104-105.

9. Wimmer, *Fasting in the New Testament*, 26.

10. Knobel, *Jewish Fasts*, 50.

11. Ibid.

granted by God (Esther 9:18-32). Our fast then especially joins us to those who have suffered for the Faith: not only those of the past, but also of the present. Many believers are victims of *in*voluntary fasting, because of their faith, resulting even in starvation since, "whenever God's Word has come forth, hard times have almost always come with it". Commenting on Matthew 9:15 Luther says,

> this is the fasting that is true to the Gospel. By our voluntary fasting, we are drawn closer to those who suffer, and ultimately to the suffering Christ, who they embody.[12]

We join in fellowship "with the departed through a profound sense of bereavement".[13] We are joined with the martyrs and saints of the past, and the persecuted, suffering and dying saints of the present. Incidentally, we are never closer to the deceased than in the celebration of the Lord's Supper where, "with angels and archangels and with *all the company of heaven* we join in the unending hymn . . . " In our fasting and suffering, we are joined with their death as part of the one crucified Body of our Lord. In the Holy Eucharist, we are joined with their life as part of the same resurrected Body of our Lord. Our periods of fasting then affect the rest of the year when we do not fast by changing our attitudes about what it means to be a Christian;[14] that our Faith is not about physical prosperity and blessing which is often absent amongst the suffering saints. Because of its connection with persecution, the Fathers perceived fasting as the exclusive privilege of the Christian.[15] In our voluntary fasts we are joined with those who have undergone involuntary fasts even unto death.

In this sense, one could argue that fasting is simply what Christians already do when they suffer. After all, suffering always accompanies life lived under the cross of Christ: daily we kill the old Adam, we approach our own death and we fight a painful war with our own flesh, as well as bearing

---

12. AE 46:235.

13. Block, *The Biblical and Historical background of Jewish Customs and Ceremonies*, 170.

14. Knobel, *Jewish Fasts*, 147.

15. Therefore, "the Jews add new sins to old by their fasting" (Pomerius, *Ancient Christian Writers*, 98). It belongs to believers only and the Lord is blasphemed when fasting is practiced by others who do it as a work or righteousness. Commenting on the Jewish fast as an abomination, St. Chrysostom states (based on Is 58:4-5): "if your fasting was an abomination when you were striking your fellow slaves, does it become acceptable now that you have slain your Master? How could that be right?" (Chrysostom, *Discourses against Judaizing Christians*, 9)

the consequences of the assaults of sin, death and the devil. Luther said that the Christian life can be characterized by three activities: they pray (*oratio*), they meditate (*meditatio*), and they suffer (*tentatio*). These three facets of the Christian life all come together in fasting. Whenever we suffer, we are already fasting!

Fasting's connection to suffering sheds some light on the following words of Luther in his letter *Against Hanswurst*:

> Yet someone might say, 'You lack one thing, namely, fasting, because you heretics do not fast (they say). Lord God, if there is one thing we have from the ancient church, it is unfortunately fasting. If there is one thing the papists have from the new church, it is that they do not fast but live riotously and on fast days even more than on feast days. Indeed, we do not just fast, but (with St. Paul in 1 Cor 4:11) we suffer hunger. We see it daily in our poor ministers, their wives and children, and in many other poor people, whose hunger stares at you out of their eyes . . . The papists laugh at this, but they only prove thereby that *we are the ancient church suffering scorn and injury at the hands of the children of the devil*.[16] (italics mine)

Congruently, fasting prepares us for these promised hard times, the days of coming persecution, by helping us not to rely on the created things like food (especially all the delicacies of the North American diet!) and instead to rely on the Creator who can never be taken away from us. This is the *real* fast whereby fasting "from necessity and to suffer scorn, pious preachers are not given a piece of bread".[17] Fasting is a discipline that helps us prepare for those hard days ahead. Luther makes this similar point about secular fasts:

> A secular or civil fast, by the government is practical: fasting in good times to save for hard times. It teaches people to live a little more moderately, especially those who are young, sturdy, and strong.[18]

By fasting we prepare ourselves for the storms to come so that we can more fully participate in the beatific vision beyond:

> Let us also prepare for the day that we are *spiritually deprived* by the anti-Christ. Real fasting of Christians means that you punish your whole body and compel it, as well as all five senses, to forsake

---

16. AE 41:198-199.
17. AE 21:161.
18. AE 21:159.

> and do without whatever makes life comfortable. This may be either voluntary or compulsory. You may eat either fish or meat, but no more than your real need requires.[19] (italics mine)

Another 'practical' function of fasting is that it teaches us to carry the divine liturgy into our weekday routine, as our Sabbath rest is not confined merely to a couple of hours on a Sunday morning.

> It is an outward Christian discipline and exercise for the young and simple people, by which they can learn to keep track of the seasons and make the proper distinctions throughout the year.[20]

The believer is better able to reflect on the meaning of events in the Church year, and experience their significance in a bodily way. It is unfortunate that in North American Christianity, fasting has all but disappeared, and along with it, opportunities to taste and remember the bitterness of our Lord's passion. When we attempt to imitate Christ's fast, we appreciate more fully the hardships that He underwent when He fasted forty days in the desert as part the process of salvation—which centers entirely around His works and not ours!—as we pray in The Litany. In fact, the catechetical nature of this forty day fast is driven home by church traditions that observed a more "manageable" six-day period that included some dry food, bread, salt and water.[21] The intent of fasting is not to imitate Christ as if we could achieve what He did, but to learn from Him! And the Lenten fast avails us the best opportunity. If fasting were never practiced except for one time in the year, the Lenten season would be the most appropriate time as it not only connects us with Christ and our family of the past—by the correlation of forty days and forty years (Num 14:34) of the Israelites and Christ in the desert—but also our family of the present[22] and future. Augustine says

---

19. AE 21:161.
20. AE 21:159.
21. Chemnitz, *Examination of the Council of Trent IV*, 377.
22. The statutory fast on Good Friday came from the Quartodeciman Controversy. The Quartodeciman adopted the anti-Jewish practice of fasting during the feast of Passover and celebrating Easter the following day. When the date of Easter came to be determined independently of the Jewish calendar, always on a Sunday, the conditions were established for the institution of a public Christian fast on the preceding Friday. Eventually, as baptisms were normally celebrated at Easter, partial abstinence during the preceding weeks of the preparation began to be observed not only by the candidates, but also by all Church members as an annual Lenten fast of penitence (Freedman, *Isaiah II*, 776).

that even those who are "sluggish at other times are aroused to fast during Lent."[23] Furthermore,

> The forty day fast then is in fact a symbol of Lent signifying the life of the present world, just as Easter prefigures eternal bliss. The sadness of Lent prepares us for the rejoicing at Easter.[24]

Lenten fasting enlightens us on the proper relationship between Good Friday and Easter, repentance and forgiveness, confession and absolution, Law and Gospel. Just as our kingdom on earth is a miniature of the Kingdom of heaven, our Church year is a miniature of Christological history.

> For Christians, receiving food is an act of thanksgiving and experiencing the world as a gift. Yet, abstaining from food is a confession that the world is not the source of life. The feast is a sign of the joyful Kingdom, while fasting declares that Kingdom in the absence of the Bridegroom.[25]

In this sense fasting is eschatological. We continue to fast in the absence of the Bridegroom [see Appendix II], reminding us that although we exist in the 'already', we also exist in the 'not yet'; doubling as a time of sadness and waiting, and a time of joy and rest.

> For when Christ ascends to heaven and is removed from our sight, we suffer hunger not of body but of love, and we are burdened not so much by want of food as by desire.[26]

Like candles decorating window sills during the holy season of Advent, fasting expresses the Bride of Christ's eager anticipation for the homecoming of her beloved husband. Fasting prepares us for His second advent; it prepares us also for death—whichever comes first. Therefore, in *Word and Sacrament* we are taught that,

> fasting is aimed at holding down the Old Adam, suppressing the sinful nature, accustoming it to do without all that is pleasing for this life, and thus *preparing it more and more each day for death*, so that the work and purpose of baptism may be fulfilled.[27] (italics mine)

---

23. Augustine, *Sermons on Liturgical Seasons*, 86.
24. Caesarius of Arles, *Sermons*, 49.
25. Papathanassiou, *Christian Fasting in Postmodern Society*, 256.
26. Maximus, *Sermons*, 110.
27. AE 35:34.

The Church on earth and all creation waits in eager anticipation for the Resurrection of the dead. In fasting we individual believers learn about the Resurrection of the body, specifically the relationship to Holy Baptism. To emphasize this intimate relationship, St. Patrick (390-460), bishop and catholic missionary to the Irish, encouraged catechumens to undergo baptism during the Easter Vigil, after the candidate underwent a forty day fast.[28] Accordingly, St. Augustine says,

> he who strives in a contest abstains from all things, but food is proper in the hope of peace which will not be achieved until our body, whose redemption we hope for, will have put on immortality. However, we now feast by anticipation upon that glory which we do not yet take by actual possession. St. Paul predicted our doing both these things at the same time when he said: "rejoicing in hope, patient in tribulation" (Rom.12:12), as if the former were contingent on God; the latter, on fasting. In fact, when we enter upon the way of the Lord, let us fast from the vanity of this present life, and refresh ourselves with the hope of the future life, not focusing our heart on things here, but feasting it on things above.[29]

We recall how Luther was not a great fan of the forty-day Lenten fast, evidenced in his comments on the Gospel of St. John in which he harshly accuses it (perhaps falsely) as being "introduced by heretics".[30] Yet his hostility was directed towards abuse, how its true purpose was lost amongst self-righteous monks. By creating a long list of compulsory fasts, these Christians presented themselves as holier than the laypeople. They also constructed fasts that were easily attainable to fulfill, failing to appreciate the purpose of a true God-pleasing fast:

> They call it fasting if you abstain from eating meat; but meanwhile you may eat the finest fish with the most expensive sauces and spices and strongest wines![31]

Instead Luther advises,

> general spiritual fasts for us Christians [are those observed] for a few days before Easter, before Pentecost and before Christmas, to distribute fasts over the year. But on no account dare it be done for

---

28. Patrick, *Ancient Christian Writers*, 53;98.
29. Augustine, *Sermons on Liturgical Seasons*, 396.
30. AE 24:228.
31. AE 21:158.

> the purpose of making it an act of worship or a means of meriting something and reconciling God . . .[32]

Like all ascetic acts, fasting must be understood correctly in order for it to build faith up and not destroy it. Luther's *ad hominem* argument concerning mournful fasts is illuminated by Augustine's instruction "that simple foods sustain fasting, not delicacies".[33] And despite Luther's personal prejudice, there is something redeemable in the traditional forty-day fast and as Augustine advises, "we ought to humble ourselves as Christ humbled himself in proper recognition of the Lenten season".[34]

Even the symbolism of the fast is remarkable, as it points not to our acts of righteousness but to Christ's. Actually, our fasting does not demonstrate how well we do it, but how poorly. In this way, it re-focuses us on God's works instead of our own filthy rags (Isa 64:6). The term for Lent in the Eastern Church is "holy forty"[35] or "fortieth", indicating the liturgical importance of fasting in that tradition.[36] Furthermore, the Easterners recognize three other "Lents" throughout the year along with the traditional Lent.[37] The notion is so embedded in the Eastern liturgy that St. Maximus the Confessor claims that the forty bishops stand for the forty days of the Lenten fast.[38] Likewise, the bishop of Ravenna, St. Chrysologus or "Doctor of Homilies" argued that because the number is sacred, teaching us the divine affairs of God (i.e. in four and ten), the Lenten fast is a "symbolic mystery" of grace.[39] Just as the Lord's Day forces us to take a rest when we are inclined to treat every day equally, so too the liturgical year forces us to break up the patterns and rhythms of our self-made routines, and reflect upon the timeline of our Lord's instead . . . .and always for our benefit. Although Christmas has its place and purpose, no Christian would opt to stay there for the full year. Twelve days seem like enough, and visits to the Christmas stores in Frankenmuth during the summer holidays seem out of place somehow. Christian pilgrims are spiritually "hotwired" to follow the liturgical Church year: such as their journey from Advent and the holy

32. AE 21:159.
33. Augustine, *Sermons on Liturgical Seasons*, 91.
34. Ibid., 90.
35. *New Catholic Encyclopedia*, 848.
36. Maximus, *Sermons*, 198, 206.
37. *New Catholic Encyclopedia*, 848.
38. Maximus, *Sermons*, 198, 206.
39. Chrysologus, *Sermons*, 272.

incarnation at Christmas, to Christ's revelations and teachings during the seasons of Epiphany and Lent, with desperate and hopeful eyes fixed on the pinnacle of Good Friday on the mountain of Holy Week. The highest peak, adorned with a Roman cross, casts a ceaseless shadow on this circular footpath, a narrow mountain pass that spirals up with sights towards its final plateau of eternal rest and heavenly peace. Each step of the way along this sometimes difficult and uncomfortable route compels us to behave, think and react differently. Years ago, I experienced the pains and pleasures of a traditional Turkish bath in Ephesus. The spa consisted of various chambers through which I passed: from soothing hot baths to extreme cold showers, steam rooms to saunas, to large hairy men scrubbing clients with a dry prickly sponge. My feelings vacillated between those of delight to those of sheer terror. But at the end, I was so relaxed and calm that it resulted in one of the most wonderful sleeps in my life. The Church year takes us into chambers in which we would rather not pass, but the results are always "very good" indeed. And that churchly liturgy is not intended to be confined to Sunday mornings, but demands us to incorporate it into the "propers" and "ordinaries" of our homes in worship and the rubrics of the rhythms of our daily lives. The Sundays of Lent are mini-Easter celebrations when they presume that the faithful are fasting through the week. After all, all experiences and sentimental feelings of crucifixion lead us to the joys of resurrection. The sounds and aromas of Mom's baking for the Easter morning church potluck can be detected in the late evening solemnities of Good Friday. Even during the somber fast, we hear Mom in the kitchen, and can already smell the feast baking in the oven. All fasting looks forward to a feasting, a "'vigil' kept in an effort to prepare for the *Gottesschau* (vision of God)".[40] Likewise, the high priest of the Old Testament did not limit his movement to the space of the Temple but moved around freely among the people. From his colourful liturgical vestments emanated the continual fragrant scent of the temple incense, while the bells of his garments could be heard within the homes that he passed. The faithful joyfully welcomed this sacred presence in the midst of them, while the unrepentant hid their spiritual nakedness from him, seeking to avoid the judgement of God. It continues to this day, with those avoiding their pastors, the Divine Service, and even the fellowship of other Christians entirely, while others seek out such visits with God. Christians are, after all, the "aroma" of Christ (2

---

40. Larin, *Feasting and Fasting According to the Byzantine Typikon*, 142.

Cor 2:15); stirring up a mixed reaction from other people, though always a pleasing fragrance to God.

Though confined to the sphere of speculation, such observation underscores the fact that when fasting during the Lenten season our bodies are mystically joined to the continuity of Christendom,[41] in much the same way as do our minds when we weekly recite the Creed and liturgy together as one body. At the very least fasting removes us from our routines and

> from the inevitable hustle-and-bustle of everyday life to enter into the reality of the church's feast and truly celebrate . . . it is to enable us to leave aside our individual cares and join in the communal celebration in and as church: as one body, one heart, one mind.[42]

When viewed through the lenses of catechesis, the sacramental character of fasting loses some of its fuzziness. Still, unclarity remains. Yet by slowly peeling away its various layers, we have gained glimpses of a priceless hidden pearl, containing the greatest lesson of all: the Eucharistic Fast.

---

41. Augustine, *Sermons on Liturgical Seasons*, 83-84.
42. Larin, *Feasting and Fasting According to the Byzantine Typikon*, 133.

8

THE EUCHARISTIC FAST

FASTING IS A GREAT educator. But above all else, fasting teaches us about the Bread from heaven and prepares us for its reception. And so, from early on, Christians fasted before reception of the Eucharist. By the fourth century it was virtually universal. They called it: "The Eucharistic Fast".

Historically a Saturday fast, which replaced the Monday and Thursday fasts of the Jews, became a day of complete abstinence from food and drink for the clergy in preparation for Holy Communion. For the laity, a one hour abstinence prior to reception of the host was mandatory.[1] This fast was practiced by many of the earliest Christians such as the Armenians, Syrians and Greeks.[2] Because "man does not live by bread alone", the Eucharistic Fast teaches us the priority of spiritual things, which is why the Desert Fathers instructed that, "no food should be given for the flesh before providing spiritual nourishment for the soul".[3] Although not all Christians support the mandating of such rules of observance, and for good reason, there remains much value in not only understanding the meaning and appreciating the benefits of such a fast, but also in practicing it when, and only when, it is done out of Christian freedom.

The Eucharistic Fast prepares a Christian for the reception of God's Word made flesh. The Bible records several instances of people abstaining

1. *New Catholic Encyclopedia*, 847.
2. Anglin, *The Eucharistic Fast*, 24.
3. Russell, *The Lives of the Desert Fathers*, 64.

from food in preparation for the reception of God's Word whether that be for instruction, direction or wisdom. In Acts 13:2-3 we hear how fasting and prayer preceded a divine call or ordination amongst the leaders of the Church at Antioch as they sought God's divine direction. This was also common in the Old Testament. II Chronicles 20:3 describes fasting among the people of Judah asking for help and advice before a battle. Likewise, the Old Testament prophets were often in the process of fasting when God revealed His message to them. Daniel was fasting when he received his famous visions (9:2 f; 10:2-3,12). We are also told of the story of Joseph in the pseudepigrapha who received a mystical experience while fasting (T Jos III: 1-5).[4] Some Christians practiced fasting as preparatory for receiving the Word by doing it before Vespers, None and other orders of the Office. Many wholesome Christian practices have a corrupted and demonic counterpart in other religions. The Eucharistic Fast is no exception. Fasting was practiced as a means of preparing for intercourse with the deity and for the reception of ecstatic or magical powers,[5] shadowing the Eucharistic Fast which is, indeed, an intimate communion between the heavenly Bride and Groom, the Church and Jesus Christ, which insurmountably surpasses the intimacy of any sexual relationship.[6]

4. Wimmer, *Fasting in the New Testament*, 10.
5. Kittel, *The Theological Dictionary of the New Testament*, 926.
6. The preparation for divine communication is also echoed in the practices of other religions, although, again, they embrace a corrupt understanding of the practice. Herodotus speaks of fasts which priests had to observe in Egypt before entering the sanctuary, offering sacrifices or performing cultic acts (Kittel, *The Theological Dictionary of the New Testament*, 926), which was supposed to make one fit for the presence of a deity. Related to the role of fasting and spiritual warfare, the *taanit chalom* of the Jews was "a dream fast" said to prevent materialization of nightmares in the future (Bloch, *The Biblical and Historical background of Jewish Customs and Ceremonies*, 352).

The Greeks and Romans believed that abstention made one receptive to ecstatic revelations (Kittel, *The Theological Dictionary of the New Testament*, 927), experiences which can be explained with psychological reasons as well as spiritual ones; visions and ecstatic experiences can be expected when one is in such a weak state and with a weakened mind. Secular literature also argues that mental sharpness often comes during long periods without solid food (Berry, *Fasting Safely*, 2). The psychological argument does explain for *some* experiences such as this prescription for the Talmudic Rabbis of the first and second centuries:

> Jewish mystical tradition centered on contemplation on the vision of the *Merkavah*, the heavenly chariot described in the first chapter of the book of Ezekiel. The contemplators were known as the riders of the Chariot, those who engaged in soul ascents to the heavenly halls where they saw God and his

We discover the most significant example of fasting in preparation for divine communication in both Deuteronomy 9:9 and Exodus 34:28. These report Moses' fast for forty days and nights before receiving the Tables of the Law while in God's presence.

> By fasting these 40 days Moses merited to speak with God, to stand and stay with him and to receive the precepts of the Law from his hand. For although his human condition prevented him from seeing God, yet the grace of his fasting drew him into close contact with the Divinity... he is more familiar, intimate and friendly with the person in whom he sees his works... by 40 day fasts God is appeased, the heavens opened and hell is shut... Therefore we too, beloved brethren, ought to fast continually and devotedly in this space of time so that the Lord might be propitiated by us, the heavens opened to us, and hell not prevail.[7]

Although St. Maximus seems to place a disproportionate emphasis on our act of fasting rather than on God's act of giving, one thing we learn is this: fasting in preparation for divine communion can be appropriate during those holy times when, and holy places where, God most intimately touches us with His glorious presence. Unsurprisingly, the Christian Wednesday and Friday fasts were traditionally followed by meditating on God's Word, prayer and, most importantly, reception of the Lord's Supper.[8] If the people of Judah, during the reign of Jehoiakim, fasted before the reading of the scroll (Jer 36:9-1) in preparation of the presence of the Holy God and His inseparable holy Word, is it not even more appropriate to fast in prepara-

---

holy angels. [This was their technique]. "You may perhaps know that many of the Sages hold that when a man is worthy and blessed with certain qualities and he wishes to gaze at the heavenly Chariot and the halls of the angels on high, he must follow certain exercises. He must fast for a specified number of days, he must place his head between his knees, whispering softly to himself certain praises of God with his face towards the grounds. As a result, he will gaze in the innermost recesses of his heart and it will seem as if he saw the seven halls with his own eyes, moving from hall to hall to observe that which is therein to be found (Jones, *The Study of Spirituality*, 493).

Exaggerated asceticism may be what is warned against in Colossians 2:8 as "self-humiliation" along with angel worship and inducing visions of angels (1 Tim 4:8)(Freedman, *Isaiah II*, 776). The writer opposes fasting when done for these reasons since bodily training is valuable only insofar as it leads us to Christ and away from self.

7. Maximus, *Sermons*, 85-86.
8. Chemnitz, Martin. *Examination of the Council of Trent IV*, 377.

tion of the ultimate 'divine communication': the Holy Communion—the *visible* Word of God—before receiving with our mouths the Word which has become (and remained) flesh, and even in earshot of the holiest of words, "This is my body given for you"? Just as we humbly bend our bodies in genuflection, we humbly bend our souls in fasting. It was good and right for Moses to fast in the presence of the Lord while receiving the Law. Is it not much more fitting to fast in the presence of the Lord while receiving the Gospel? How many Christians unwittingly fast in an unhealthy manner when they neglect to receive the Eucharist often? Thus, Jesus says that His disciples will fast when the Bridegroom is taken away from them, yet "can the wedding guests mourn [and fast] as long as the Bridegroom is with them?" (Matt 9:15)[see also Appendix II] One feasts in the presence of God. The famine felt in fasting sets the appetite of the soul for this "feast of victory" for our God, as we sing in one of the Church's Divine Services. "Is it not significant that the first sin in the human race involved eating? And is it not significant that in the New Jerusalem believers will eat from the once-protected Tree of life?"[9] If "you are what you eat", then just as our nature has been poisoned by our eating of the forbidden fruit in the Garden of Eden, a new "divinized" nature is established and displayed in the eating of the fruit of the Holy Cross of Jesus: His very Body and Blood. Although we continually feel the indigestion inherited from our forefathers' appetite for the Tree of the Knowledge of Good and Evil, we nourish ourselves on another tree: the Tree of Life in heaven from which we nibble Sunday after Sunday whenever we commune in faith. Doubting the presence of that which has been concealed from our sight is typical of our sinful nature and betrays our lack of maturity and imagination. But if we were to behold the glory contained in the feast spread before us on the Lord's table, we would beg for mercy. God is generous and knows our limitations. When He is seemingly absent, He is usually more present than we could believe to be true. He is always truly present in the Sacrament of the Altar. But just as the disciples were required to leave the Mount of Transfiguration after experiencing the Glory of God, so too, we exit the church and descend from the mountain of Mass on Sundays and re-enter the desert, with fasting.

The fast from earthly food to better feast on heavenly food teaches us patience and contentment[10] during the moments of His corporal absence—after the Mass is complete. The paths of our hearts are "made straight" for

---

9. Berghuis, *A Biblical Perspective on Fasting*, 96.
10. Wimmer, *Fasting in the New Testament*, 44.

the unique physical and spiritual strengthening (Acts 27:33) that is received in His real and physical presence. We learn to trust that God will take care of us even when He appears distant and invisible. St. Cyril of Jerusalem (315-386), famous for his *Catechetical Lectures*, teaches us this:

> For we fast by abstaining from wine and flesh, not because we abhor them as abominations but because we expect the reward, that by scorning sensible things, we may enjoy a spiritual and invisible table and that, though we now 'sow in tears', we shall reap rejoicing (Psalm 125) in the world to come.[11]

Reverently abstaining from the wine and flesh of a common supper prepares us for the wine and Flesh of the Lord's Supper. This particular function of fasting was so highly regarded amongst the medieval Catholics that it was introduced as Law in the Roman Catholic Church. Although such legalism is inexcusable as a violation of Christian freedom, it was well intended: it was meant to prevent the abuse of the Sacrament and increase reverence.[12] Although there was no Biblical precedent for the decision, the ecclesiastical Law was founded upon the natural Law of showing reverence towards holy things (1 Cor 11).[13] It logically followed that if the Lord's Body and Blood is the holiest of things, it deserves the greatest revering, demonstrated by fasting. Specifically, the fast was prescribed amongst the medieval Catholics according to the rule of St. Thomas which sought a mandatory Eucharistic fast for the following reasons: 1. the Eucharist, being holy, should enter only the mouth which is not contaminated by any other food or drink; 2. the Eucharist signifies our devotion to Christ above all and therefore the Eucharistic fast best increases this awareness of Christ as first in our heart as He is our first and most holy nourishment; 3. the Eucharistic fast prevented the possibility of vomiting out the holy food due to prior indulgence in other foods.[14] These reasons certainly reflect a high regard for the Sacrament and increase reverence. Although arguably extreme reasoning, the seriousness of the Sacramental confession of the real presence amongst these medieval believers is unquestionable and can be likened to Luther's consecrationalist view of the Lord's supper juxtaposed with the Philipist, receptionist one.

Some of the medieval followers of Carmelite friar and priest, St. John of the Cross, made the Eucharist their only source of nourishment, while

11. Cyril of Jerusalem, *Works*, 132.
12. Anglin, *The Eucharistic Fast*, 3.
13. Ibid.
14. Ibid., 4.

citing the example of the Israelites, who exclusively ate Manna in the desert, as their precedent. They wanted to avoid the Israelites' mistakes. They "longed not after earthly food" (I Enoch 108:7-9). Rather, they fasted in the spirit of these words of their leader:

> [The] Scripture . . . states that, discontented with that simple food, the [Israelites] craved and requested meat, and seriously angered our Lord because of their desire to commingle a food so base and coarse with one so high and simple, which, even though simple, contained the savor and substance of all foods (Nm 11:4; 6:10). For God thought it shameful for them to crave other food while he was giving them heavenly food . . . The Israelites did not perceive the tastes, contained in the manna, of every other food, because their appetite was not restricted to this manna . . . [15]

Yet even amongst such seemingly rigid Sacramentalists, these strict rules were not as absolute as they first sound, since exceptions were made to those who were sick,[16] reminding us that Christians have always viewed the Eucharistic fast as something done for our sake, and not for God's sake or for its own sake. It is meant to heighten the piety of The Holy Communion and make it more meaningful to us, and not God, since God forgives the sin of the believer who may on a rare occasion vomit the host out of his mouth, as He does the sin of he who accidentally spills some consecrated wine on his shirt. And so, we fast out of gratitude as well. After all, "Eucharist" means "Thanksgiving".

Incidentally, the Jews publicly practiced gratitude fasts, such as celebrating their escape from the tenth plague in Egypt. Yet the Jewish fast of the first born, like the fast of the early Church before Christmas (in devotion to the Christ child), more explicitly echoed the gift of Christ's coming[17] and, therefore, naturally included a dimension of thanksgiving (for what God will do, has done, and will continue to do). We, too, fast out of gratitude and respect for what God has so graciously done for us. All fasting helps us to better focus on Him over and above all other things and leads us to desire Him to fill up our hungry selves. The Lord is not only the one who feeds the hungry and gives drink to the thirsty but is Himself our food and

---

15. John of Cross, *Selected Writings*, 70-71.
16. Anglin, *The Eucharistic Fast*, 3-4.
17. Sullivan, *Fast and Abstinence in the First order of St. Francis*, 27.

drink. Our empty, grumbling stomachs help us to remember whose bread we eat and give thanks to God.[18] So Luther says in the *Small Catechism*:

> Fasting and bodily preparation are a good external discipline, but he is truly worthy and well prepared who believes these words, "given and shed for you for the forgiveness of sins".[19]

Our spiritual lives should by no means be distracted by our fasts. If they harm our faith or lead us to believe that we become worthier or purified by them, we should forego them. But when they lead us to grasp the unique and exceptional beauty of God's grace more wholly and in a right spirit we should love and adore them. And so, the *Large Catechism* states that

> fasting and prayer and the like may have their place as an external preparation and children's exercise so that one's body may behave properly and reverently toward the body and blood of Christ. But what is given in and with the sacrament cannot be grasped and appropriated by the body.[20]

The tradition of fasting before the Eucharist ought not be treated in a legalistic manner but considered helpful in the strengthening and deepening of our faith. Luther quoting St. Augustine in *Word and Sacrament* reminds us of this:

> But what will they say to the word which St. Augustine writes to Janarius in Epistle 118: 'It is clear that the first time the disciples received the body and blood of the Lord, they did not receive it fasting. But it pleased the Holy Spirit that in honor of so great a sacrament the Lord's body should enter the mouth of the Christian before any other food'?[21]

Although the Eucharistic Fast was a later Christian tradition, it should not be neglected as it was established for our spiritual support, presuming it is properly understood. In spite of some abuse it remains a good and useful gift. And just as our fasting body hungers for food, so our souls emptied by sin and the trials of life, hunger to be filled by the Lord: "As a deer pants for flowing streams, so pants my soul for you" (Ps 42:1).

---

18. Maximus, *Sermons*, 177.
19. SC: *Sacrament of the Altar*.
20. LC: *The Lord's Supper*.
21. AE 37:105.

Our bodies are emptied to be filled by God, in order that we feed the inner man so that the outer man can persevere in discipline.[22] Some may argue that this sounds a lot like neo-Gnostic Dualism, which the Christian Church rejects, like the Greek myths which taught that food polluted the spirit since evil spirits were believed to have inhabited certain foods. Accordingly, they believed that eating influenced dreams and the experience of oracles of the divine world.[23] Yet the Christian practice is always didactic, teaching the correct relationship of the body to soul. The immense power and significance of symbolic acts in helping us better understand our identity, our relationship with God, and His means of gracious communication with us is indicated in these wise words of Moses:

> He humbled you . . . causing you to hunger and then feeding you with manna, *to teach you* that man does not live on bread alone but on every word that comes from the mouth of the Lord (Deut 8:3)(italics mine).

Liturgically, the fourth petition of the Lord's Prayer ("give us this day our daily bread") is "acted out" in the Fast and answered in the Eucharist.

To summarize, the Eucharistic fast is never an end in itself. Jesus always *breaks* our fast with His corporal flesh for our spiritual consumption. The Eucharist truly is a "break-fast" and can be paralleled with the morning appearance of Jesus to His fasting and mourning disciples in the boat after the Resurrection. Jesus breaks their fast on that happy day (John 21:12,15). There is no need to fast in the presence of Jesus, when He visits us in the flesh [see Appendix II], while He enters our mouths and joins Himself with us mystically in the Sacrament of the Altar. Therefore, the Eucharistic service always ends the fast,[24] which begins again in His physical absence[25] (i.e. when the Eucharistic service is complete),[26] an eschatological reminder that only in heaven will we be united with Christ permanently, in the eternal Supper of the divine Lamb. On the other hand, it is also a reminder of Christ's continual sacramental and spiritual presence in our lives and bodies which are His temple and tabernacle—through a "divine blood-exchange" that transfigures us sinners back into His likeness—for

---

22. Augustine, *Sermons on Liturgical Seasons*, 83-84.
23. Wimmer, *Fasting in the New Testament*, 24.
24. Hunter, *Preaching in the Patristic Age*, 40.
25. Although Jesus is with us always by His Spirit, He is not with us in the same way, according to the same tangible mode of the Eucharist.
26. Anglin, *The Eucharistic Fast*, 33.

He sends us back into the broken world to be His wounded hands and speak His words to a hurting people. The Fathers taught us to live a life of fasting, like Anna (Luke 2:36-37) which is essentially equivalent to serving others, breaking only for the moments in which God serves us, like in the Eucharist. Only then can we appreciate these words of St. Francis: "[t]he heart becomes so filled with spiritual delights that it becomes penance for him to partake of material food."[27]

The Eucharistic Fast recognizes the presence of God among and with us, yet that presence is not exclusively manifested in the Eucharist itself. Although we encounter Jesus in a special and most intimate way in the Eucharist, we encounter him in other ways as well.[28] And so fasting is appropriate in preparation for these other encounters. For instance, we encounter Jesus in prayer.[29] The most simple and beautiful of prayers is the *Jesus prayer*—"Lord Jesus Christ, Son of God, have mercy on me a sinner"—which incidentally claims to benefit the one who prays in much the same ways as the Eucharist does the one who fasts. Commenting on the *Jesus prayer*, St. Seraphim of Sarov says,

> in order to receive Christ's light in the heart, one must withdraw from all visible things. When the soul has been purified by repentance, one must 'close the eyes of the body', and by invoking the name, be filled with light.

Some of the same things can be said about fasting. The Jesus prayer serves as "food when hungry", as "drink when thirsty", as "rest when weary", as "protection against wolves and dangers".[30] Fasting prepares us for the reception of these promises in Holy Communion. Fasting, like this ancient prayer, brings one into "the practice of the presence of God", as the faster/prayer is reminded of his own hunger and the hunger of the world as the

---

27. Sullivan, *Fast and Abstinence in the First order of St. Francis*, 53.

28. Gillet, *The Jesus Prayer*, 77.

29. For psychological reasons, secular literature argues that mental sharpness comes during long periods without solid food (Berry, *Fasting Safely*, 2) and so fasting would foster devotion and better reactivity of the mind as "they take strength away from limbs but add a bring sheen to consciences" (Caesarius of Arles, *Fathers of the Church*, 42-45). Although there may be truth in this, it does not represent the whole picture. There is a mystical aspect to fasting and prayer that passes beyond human systems and materialist explanations.

30. Gillet, *The Jesus Prayer*, 82.

faster/prayer takes the fasting/prayer into home, school, work, play: praying without ceasing; fasting without ceasing.[31]

Yet the most common encounter with Jesus is when we meet Him in other people reflected in the Benedict rule, "all guests coming into the monastery are to be received as Christ"[32] causing monks to break their fast in honour of their guest.[33]

> Jesus, who after the Resurrection chose several times to appear to his disciples "in another form" (Mark 16:12) (the unknown traveller on the road to Emmaus, the gardener near the tomb, the stranger standing on the shore of the lake), continues to meet us in our daily life in a veiled way and to confront us with this all-important aspect of his presence: his presence in man. What we do to the least of our brethren, we do to him. Under the faces of men and women we are able, with our eyes of faith and love, to see the face of the Lord; by attending to the distress of the poor, of the sick, or sinners, of all men, we put our finger on the place of the nails, thrust our hands into his pierced side, and experience personally the Resurrection and the real presence (not to be confused with essence) of Christ in his mystical body; and so we can say with St. Thomas, "my Lord and my God" (John 20:28).[34]

This is especially true when we encounter true brothers and sisters in Christ, those in whom the actual Flesh and Blood of our Lord is mystically joined with their actual flesh and blood.[35] There remains a mysterious and inexpressible joy in constantly finding our absent Bridegroom in the presence of the other[36] [see Appendix II]. Dietrich Bonhoeffer (1906-1945), the German Lutheran theologian (who was executed by the Nazis for his attempt to assassinate Adolph Hitler) says something similar in *Life Together* when describing the presence of God in the reality of the other person, offering us a reason to feast: by entertaining our neighbour, we entertain God, in whom He is hidden. We would all do well to reflect upon that profound insight the next time we invite a guest over for supper! It may not change the menu, but it will definitely change our conversation and attitude. In this

---

31. Ibid., 89.
32. Pelikan, *The Illustrated Jesus Through the Centuries*, 119.
33. Adalbert de Vogüé, *The Rule of Saint Benedict*, 259.
34. Ibid., 99.
35. It should then not surprise us that Luther notes that the Lord's Supper has both spiritual *and physical* consequences on the faithful recipient.
36. Adalbert de Vogüé, *The Rule of Saint Benedict*, 236.

sense, the mealtime prayer, "Come Lord Jesus, be our Guest, and let these gifts to us be blessed", is answered in such visits.

If fasting merely teaches discipline as an end in itself, it is of no great value. It is better to have a lower temper when around other people, than to have perfect discipline in food intake. Fasting is not meant to replace brotherly love but is instrumental in helping develop other virtues; it is not a virtue in itself.[37] Like the Benedictines, the desert abbots were accustomed to breaking their fasts when guests would unexpectedly visit, because for them they were in the midst of God himself (in the 1 John 4 sense), finding God in the "least of these" for "the children of the bridegroom do not fast while the bridegroom is with them, but only when he is taken from them, then they shall fast".[38] Not only did some of these monks eat only the Eucharistic bread as their sole source of nourishment[39] as a public proclamation of their sole nourishment in the Eucharist, and a private questioning as to why one would eat regular food when the real presence of Christ from heaven is sweeter food than any from the ground, but they were the same monks who readily recognized the presence Christ in the presence of others. "When Christ is in our presence in the fellowship with others, we should feast with them and begin our fasting when we are alone".[40]

They deemed fasting a private practice of discipline (and therefore rebuked fasting for show[41]) in order that the Christian would become a better lover and servant of brethren and not a better lover of self. Acknowledging Christ's presence among us in this way ignites a desire in the heart of the Christian to both fast always *and* feast always. After all, we remain simultaneously sinners and saints who feed continually on the Paschal Bread, until we dine eternally at the Lamb's high feast in our heavenly and glorious home of the New Jerusalem.

37. Waddell, *The Desert Fathers*, 152.
38. Ibid., 114.
39. Russell, *The Lives of the Desert Fathers*, 93.
40. Waddell, *The Desert Fathers*, 114.
41. Ibid., 91.

Conclusion

Usually when Christians approach the subject of fasting, they are tempted to limit its meaning and purpose to a means of demonstrating to God their seriousness about a certain petition. This is not an unreasonable view. But fasting encompasses much more than just that. A diamond is beautiful to gaze upon from a distance. But the fullness of its glory is only revealed from a closer position. Only after drawing one's eye towards it, deliberately and intensely, with, say, the help of a jeweler's loupe, do the complex relationships between its shapes and angles—and how they are marvellously united in their reflection of light—become apparent. Similarly, to appreciate the multifaceted dimensions of fasting's splendour, takes some effort, but is well worth while. And unlike a diamond, that one simply *observe*s, fasting is best appreciated when *practiced*. For God is not only our jewel but in Holy Baptism we have become His (Matt 13:45-46). Otherwise, we are tempted to fragment fasting, as many religious fasters who unknowingly abuse this most excellent gift have done, by reducing its value to a pragmatic formula: "This does that". Instead fasting is one sacramental expression of the Christian Faith, interconnected with all the others, as together they pivot around the Sacraments proper, deriving their meaning and beauty from this one central source. In fact, fasting fuses many features of the Christian life into one pious act. It involves: a call to meditation and intercession; a realization of the Presence of God; a sacrificial offering of the heart; a sharing in the joy and strength of the Resurrection; a transfiguration of all men and all things.[1] The Holy Scriptures, sacred tradition and saints of both past and present, teach us a great deal about the subject. Yet the greatest lesson must culminate in fasting as a lifelong attitude, a

---

1. Gillet, *The Jesus Prayer*, 90.

CONCLUSION

constant recognition of our dependence on God's grace in Jesus Christ, especially as we come to Him—or rather He comes to us—in the His Holy Supper. It is in this truth that the sacramental character of fasting is most fully revealed in the sacramental life.

Despite every endeavour to unpack the profound meaning of fasting, ambiguity and mystery continue to surround it. And, so, our journey has disclosed a definite mystical character to fasting, not just in the Eucharistic fast, but in general. The Desert Fathers were some of the most renown fasters, and although some of these early Christians may err on the side of works righteousness—may God have mercy on us when we fall into this temptation as, in some form or other, we do throughout the day—they have great spiritual wisdom to offer today's Christian. Their discussions of the practice of fasting in relation to God and others is illuminating and edifying and offers an appropriate end to this discussion. The fasting of these ascetics embodied all of the reasons for our fasts.

Although these monks focused primarily on the idea that worldly desires and appetites ought to be subdued and that fasting helps us control our passions in the long run, fasting became important to them for deeper reasons. Fasting reveals those things that really matter. Fasting teaches us to rely solely upon the only one who can truly satisfy our needs, nourishing us at His table with His own Flesh and Blood. By failing to be reminded of our complete dependence on God, our precious identity as God's children, made so in the priceless waters of Holy Baptism, is at stake.

The more we fast, the more we are aware of the truth of our identity in Christ as members of His Body of which He is the Head. As strange as it may sound, when we lose sight of fasting as an attitude, we can actually end up gorging on a fast, or become gluttons in our abstentions. Both acts of eating and fasting can be driven by a greedy and twisted desire to satisfy our needs by our own deeds; a self-indulgence on our own acts of piety, regardless of how sincere they may be. When the abbot Joseph asked the abbot Pastor, "How should I fast?" the abbot Pastor said, "I would have it so that every day one should deny one's self a little in eating, so as not to be satisfied." The abbot Joseph said to him, "But when thou was a young man, didst thou not fast two days and upwards?" And the old man said, "Two days, believe me, and three, and a week: but all these things did the great old men bring to proof: and they found that it is good to eat a little every day, and on certain days a little less: and they have shown us this master road, for it is easy and light."[2]

The spirit of fasting involves an attitude rooted in holy suffering and love for God, coupled with good works and complemented by prayer. It helps to nourish a humble soul, allowing us to recognize our constant dependence on our Creator and Provider. Our fasting opens many doors for God to provide for us spiritually, showering us with His gifts. It also opens up unexpected doors for us to pass this message on to the unbelieving world, empowering us to treat other people as if we were entertaining angels (Heb 13:2): God's presence among us. In a mystical manner, the Desert Fathers suggest that it is when we are in a state of pain that we can best experience the compassion of God.[3] They speak words of wisdom when they say, "The suffering of flesh brings peace to the soul".[4] Likewise, it is the deformity of Christ which forms us; His deformity is our comeliness; to share in His suffering is a great blessing.[5] Whenever Christians suffer they are led closer to their saviour whose sanctifying grace includes their participation in His suffering Body on earth. "He is risen, indeed, Allelulia!" and yet . . . He still suffers, through His Church, until the Final Day when He will return in glory. Italian mystic Catherine of Genoa is characterized as the saint who prayed for more afflictions even though she already suffered from a multitude of illnesses. When understood in Christian maturity, such attempts at welcoming suffering embody the notion that the holy Church is a suffering Body and wherever we encounter suffering, we encounter Christ.

When we fast always—and, remember, in Christ, we already do—we are reminded of the Gospel always. The sacraments have been described as the constant on-going rhythm of experiencing and reflecting God's grace.[6] By fasting, our attitudes are transfigured, as we see others through God's eyes, touching others with His wounded hands, encountering them as the suffering Christ.

Yet let us not shut our ears to the words of Martin Luther, the voice crying in the wilderness commanding us to repent of that fasting done in the wrong spirit and for the wrong reasons. The empty outward shell of

---

2. Waddell, *The Desert Fathers*, 103.
3. Ibid., 152.
4. Ibid., 85.
5. Pelikan, *The Illustrated Jesus Through the Centuries*, 109
6. Elliott, *The Christ Life*, 67.

religious works appears in every age and culture including our own. Luther reminds us that these religious works ought to flow out of the Christian as expressions of the faith, a sign and symbol and mark of conversion to God,[7] instead of as a rule to be obeyed. If we think that our fast (or any pious activity) is intrinsically impressive to God, we are mistaken. God says, "big deal" to all our good works when we think them something special and something about which to boast. Yet when we offer up to Him our brokenness or the brokenness of others, it is a most precious gift (Ps 51:16-17).

When fasting becomes a duty, it results not in fruit but in thorns, as was the case with the Israelites. In Isaiah's contradistinction between a true versus hypocritical fast (see Appendix I), the Holy Scriptures depict what a true fast is, not just for the Jews but also for us. Our heavenly Father appears at first to be condemning external fasting altogether. But on closer inspection, it is clear that He rejects fasting when "it wants to become a cover to blind our eyes so that we may not see our sins", in the words of Luther.[8] Instead, when we read Isaiah we can remember the Litany, that by His "baptism, *fasting* and temptation" the Redeemer was already reflecting His sacrificial character, ultimately displayed in the Passion. Jesus fasted perfectly to redeem our imperfect fasting, as part of God's assumption of human flesh. Because Christ fasted for us,[9] we have the Bridegroom with us forever.[10] Fasting cannot improve our status with God. Rather fasting is a joyful avenue with which God has graced us to help us in our faith.

7. Kittel, *The Theological Dictionary of the New Testament*, 933.

8. AE: 17, 284.

9. The position which Jesus adopts towards fasting is new and distinctive. He spent forty days and nights fasting in the wilderness in the beginning of his temptation which was already not in accordance with current practice. Behind the story obviously stands reminiscence of Moses' fast on Sinai. The way of the Messiah corresponds to that of Moses. But where the covenant mediator of the Old Testament fasted in preparation for the revelation of God, Jesus had already received and fasted in order to be equipped and confirm the Messianic dignity and power with which he had been invested (Kittel, *The Theological Dictionary of the New Testament*, 932) in the state of humiliation.

10. Fasting before God, the Father of those who turn to him, is joy. Hence there is [little] place for melancholy signs of mourning. Mark 2:18ff goes further. The immediate disciples of Jesus do not fast like the more pious of the people, the disciples of John and the Pharisees. When complaint is made about this, Jesus will not accept it. He defends the disciples claiming fasting in the presence of the Bridegroom in nonsensical. The presence of the Messiah, the time of salvation which has dawned, means joy. Sorrow and fasting belong to the time of waiting for salvation. This is true for the disciples too, who by His death will be put back into the state of waiting (Jn16:20). Seen from the standpoint of the Messianic eschatological centre of the message of Jesus, fasting is transcended. But since

Just as prayer has often been mistreated as an attempt at manipulating God to get what we want out of Him, fasting is liable to the same error. The common teaching that prayer/fasting for specific blessings assures their granting leads believers to doubt God's reliability.[11] These patterns of thought unveil the "work-holy delusion which lurks behind the self-righteous and unrighteous, concealed, revealed, exposed by God through his prophets".[12]

And, so, adopting the spirit of fasting is more important than fasting itself. We need to be reminded of the nature of a true fast in a Christian community where fasting has unfortunately all but fallen completely out of practice amongst both lay and clergy alike. It is not a religious 'hoop' through which God asks us to jump as some sort of arbitrary exercise of training or obedience. George Whitefield thought Christianity meant "going nasty".[13] St. John of the Cross counselled, "Whatever you find pleasant to the soul or body abandon; whatever is painful embrace it".[14] There certainly is value in disciplining oneself to endure hardness, but God has no satisfaction in our discomfort as an end in itself any more than He dislikes our happiness. Nineteenth-century British history, Thomas Babington Macaulay wrote that, "the puritan hated bear-baiting, not because it gave pain to the bear, but because it gave pleasure to the spectators." Such fear of the pleasant is far removed from the appreciative enjoyment of the son of man.[15]

True fasting, like true worship, means showing mercy to others by giving up some of your own pleasure for the sake of someone else. According to this definition, stewardship then is a form of fasting; almsgiving is a form of fasting; doing volunteer work is a form of fasting; giving up time in front of the television to visit a lonely neighbour is a form of fasting. Christ gave up everything for us and is pleased when we give up things for others,

---

Jesus is aware of an interval between Now and Then, between the dawn of salvation on earth and its consummation, He finds a place for fasting between the times. It is not of course a pious work. It is a sign and symbol of the inner attitude which perhaps hardly needs such a sign and symbol. The attitude of Jesus to fasting is not unlike that of the prophets. But the reasons and concrete expression are His own, uniquely determined by his Messianic consciousness (Kittel, *The Theological Dictionary of the New Testament*, 932-933).

11. Buttrick, *The Book of Isaiah*, 679.
12. Delitzsch, *The Prophecies of Isaiah III*, 387
13. Ibid., 680.
14. Ibid.
15. Ibid.

CONCLUSION

as signs of thanksgiving. And on that note, forgiving others is probably the greatest form of fasting. Whenever we forgive others who have wronged us we release the bonds that oppress them, just as God has released the bond that oppressed us when His son carried the yoke for our sake (Isaiah 58: 6). In his commentary on Zechariah in 1527, Luther pointedly states that true fasting is "forgiving your enemies . . . and doing good to them".[16]

Fasting is not a work of piety to earn God's favour but is an expression of God's Spirit active in the Christian life. Thus, it is not a Law thing, but a Gospel thing; a gift given to man from God.

> During the 40 days of Lent we ought to rest from the winds and the sea of this world by taking refuge, as it were, in the haven of Lent, and in the quiet silence to receive the divine lessons in the receptacle of our heart. [Fasting] repairs in the little ship of our soul whatever throughout the year has been broken or destroyed or damaged or ruined by many storms, that is, by the waves of sins. And since it is necessary for us to endure the storms and tempests of this world while we are still in this frail body, as often as the enemy wills to lead us astray by means of the roughest storms or to deceive us by the most voluptuous pleasure, with God's help may he always find us prepared against him.[17]

Our motivation to fast is not the Law, but the Gospel. May we joyously and thankfully, feast on His fasting, strengthened by fasting's sacramental character during every one of our spells of hunger and weakness.

---

16. AE 20:263.
17. Caesarius of Arles, *Fathers of the Church*, 42-45.

Epilogue

The Example of the Pastor

IN HIS THOUGHT-PROVOKING BOOK, *Reclaiming Patterns of Ministry: Jesus and Paul*, Dr. Jonathon Grothe discusses the subject of 'imitating Christ', demonstrating from The Holy Scriptures that St. Paul displays patterns of the ministry of Jesus, and that these patterns are paradigmatic for us as well.[1] These patterns act as a chain, by imitation and representation, from Jesus to Paul to us.[2] Pastors seek to imitate St. Paul, as he imitated Christ. Parishioners tend to imitate their pastors, who represent and embody Christ in and through the pastoral ministry. And, so, it is appropriate to search in Scripture for the

> patterns of Christ's ministry revealed in Paul [since] in Paul we have a reflection of Jesus, a mirroring of His ministry, a pattern portrayed in a number of paradigms, imitations that happen as a recipient and bearer of the Spirit.[3]

These patterns are not derived from man but from God. After all, God constructed the human being as a creature in His own image and likeness. Man acts as a mirror-reflection of His holiness and glory, created as an imitator of God.[4] The light of the Son, the chief High Priest, shines forth through the priests called to His churches by their various God-given vocations and life situations.

1. Grothe, *Reclaiming Patterns of Pastoral Ministry*, 12.
2. Ibid., 14.
3. Grothe, *Reclaiming Patterns of Pastoral Ministry*, 14-15.
4. Grothe, Reclaiming Patterns of Pastoral Ministry, 69.

EPILOGUE

I would argue that an example is found not only in our Father Paul, but in our other Fathers as well: both saints before us, and saints among us. Other pastors, perhaps even those fondly remembered from childhood, are also mentors. Subsequent pastors honour them according to the Fourth Commandment, imitating their faith and pious lives, while also covering their sins and overlooking their faults. Likewise, faith and piety of pastors are mentored by lay people who are examples of faith and confessors of the Faith to the world. Pastors are ambassadors to their people who, in turn, are ambassadors to the world (2 Cor 5:20).

Modern theologians like Henri Nouen and ancient ones like the author of the *Imitation of Christ* (attributed to Thomas á Kempis) testify to the fact that Christ mystically dwells in the pastoral office through His ministers, or *administers,* of that office. Liturgical traditions, such as the pastor's stole representing the carrying of a yoke, the priestly chasuble representing the hidden presence of our great High Priest, and even the tabs of clerical shirts representing pastors as slaves of Christ, are compelling reminders to the clergy that pastoral conduct is not to be taken lightly. It is, in fact, crucial to the office of the ministry, for "in it is preserved the concrete models of the love of God in action".[5] Ministers are, in a sense, sacraments. Even the careless ones are instruments of God's grace, teaching and proclaiming the Gospel in both word and deed. They preach the Gospel. They absolve sins. They consecrate the elements in the Holy Eucharist. They anoint with oil. They even exorcise demons. Clearly, they are images and icons of Christ who is the image and icon of God (Col 1:15).[6] Jesus promised to be with His Church always, even until the end of the age. His promise is fulfilled in the pastoral office that He Himself has established (Matt 28:16-20). The divine call and promise offered to His first disciples, continues today through the Apostolic Ministry: called and ordained ministers of His Word and Sacraments.

Icons help people worship. People learn not only from reading and hearing, but from experiencing, seeing and interacting with others. Through the artistic representations of the qualities and characteristics of the glorious saints who rest in Jesus, an icon didactically conveys the Gospel via non-auditory God-given senses such as our vision. Pastors are living icons. The Pastor's words of absolution truly forgive sins because he acts as a mouthpiece of God. In other words, he not only represents God

---

5. Ibid., 81.
6. The Greek word for "image" is "icon".

among us, but *re*-present Him, sacramentally. The comfort that a penitent sinner encounters in this personal aspect of the office when he hears the words of forgiveness as if from the mouth of God Himself, is not found in any human system. Although the exchange of words between lovers in a letter conveys no different message from that of a conversation over the telephone, hearing the voice of the lover touches the heart of the beloved in a way that gives more credibility to the message; i.e. faith in the message is strengthened. Well, the pastor, when faithful to God's Word, is that voice in the midst of his congregation. In fact, he is a tangible, living means of grace to his congregation, not by any peculiar virtue within him, but for the sake of the Gospel word of Christ. Accordingly, he, as shepherd, and those sheep to which he attends, bring glory not to himself but to the Chief Shepherd of the universal flock. A pastor is the Father, the image of Christ, the mentor to his children, acting as Christ's 'earthen vessels' among them.[7] Pastors, as part of the apostolic succession, are sent as representatives and imitators to serve and minister to God's people in Jesus' name.[8]

> At times Paul speaks of his own actions and experiences as an apostle, a specially-set-aside minister, and there comes through a hint of his suffering and dying for other's sake. Not only is the content of his preaching the Gospel of life for all through the death of Christ, but also the *conduct* of his own ministry, as an apostolic imitator of the servanthood of Jesus, conforms to the pattern in which life is brought into being through suffering and death. The self-giving love that means life for others is stamped not only on Paul's words, but also on his ministry.[9]

People 'watch' the pastor, and this can be a good thing. Events and people in the Old Testament were typological of Christ and His work. They pointed forward to Christ. The sufferings of a Pastor are typologically imitative, pointing not forward, but backward to this same Christ.[10]

> Pastors, like apostles are singled out, set aside with a specific role in ministry pertaining to their office, by divine institution, to be channels, proclaimers in word, deed, and in sufferings, of the Word of the Gospel of the crucified Christ ... They participate in, typologically reveal, imitate and so re-present in a given time and

7. Grothe, *Reclaiming Patterns of Pastoral Ministry*, 25.
8. Ibid., 32.
9. Ibid., 33.
10. Ibid., 44.

place that which was accomplished at Calvary on Good Friday for all times and places in Jesus Christ.[11]

Because pastors are examples for their people to follow in so far as they imitate Christ, St. Paul can rightly advise the Corinthians to "imitate me" without sounding egoistic or cultist (1 Cor 4:16). Pastors of the present and past act as mentors to all the faithful which is why higher standards of morality have been applied to them. Perhaps because of this very role and place in the public light, many are gifted with a special measure of grace in better fulfilling their difficult role as God's ambassadors. Christ indwells them, because of their office, in a special way, not for their own sake, but for the sake of the people. A pastor is an icon of Christ, giving his sheep a visual representation of our Lord, so that he who hears the preacher preach, or the absolver absolve, can be assured that this individual is the mouthpiece of their Good Shepherd, especially during the Divine Service. The office of the Holy Ministry is another example of how our God gives good gifts to His children and abides sacramentally amongst them. There is something to be said about the notion that the Nazarite vow in the Old Testament is not totally inapplicable to the Christian Church today. If the laity are a priesthood, the pastors represent and re-present the Office of High Priesthood, filled by Christ our great High Priest. This distinction is not a qualitative one, as if pastors are better Christians or more beloved by God, but a vocational one: imitation for the edification of God's precious and holy people (Num 6:3-4). The laity do not imitate their shepherds under Christ, the Chief Shepherd, for imitation's own sake, as a means of works righteousness or to idolize the clergy. At the very least, they imitate their faith and doctrine. Referring to the book of Hebrews, Luther writes:

> The individual works of the Holy Fathers are by no means to be taken as a pattern for everyone to imitate, the way the monks imitate the fasting of Benedict like monkeys with no understanding. Imitate the faith and not necessarily the actions of the Church Fathers.[12]

When fasting and other *ascesis* are understood correctly and increase this faith, they act as valuable patterns for the believers to imitate since "all servants and saints are characterized by fasts and show the providence of

---

11. Ibid.
12. AE 2:113.

God for His faithful servant".[13] Because faith always produces good works, imitation of both, when we encounter them in faithful pastors, is inevitable for the Lord's saints.

The *ascesis* (self-discipline) of Jesus, Paul and the other apostles, prophets, and Christian fathers serve as models of ministry. Pastors should imitate their prayer, good deeds and piety. We see the importance of fasting amongst St. Paul and many others.[14] In fasting, the faster is remade into the image of our Christ the servant as his faith is remade in the image of Christ our Lord. In the Pauline Epistles we hear that sometimes fasting is involuntary, and, at those times, is synonymous with suffering. The imitation of Jesus and Paul always includes a participation in their suffering.[15] When pastors bear this cross as suffering servants, they not only mystically encounter the Christ, but they share in the Passion. Fasting as part of the repentance process was, according to monastic theologian Peter Damian (d. 1072), "truly sharing in the passion of the Redeemer", for by it are the allurements of the flesh crucified in imitation of Christ on the cross. What Christ had suffered in Himself as the Head of the Church, He continues to suffer in His members.[16] Thus, Christian mystics have seen some value, when understood correctly and maturely, in the 'self-inflicted pain' of fasting. Fasting was understood to drive out any obstacle to be conformed to Christ's image. It was believed that to emulate Christ made one like Christ. The Franciscan monks, for instance, would actively create meals in which the food was tasteless with no flavour or bad flavour and would drink "just enough water, not enough [even] to quench their thirst". St. Francis mingled ashes with his food to keep it from being too palatable.[17] Such asceticism was according to the Franciscans a beloved mirroring of Christ. Certainly, the Franciscan practice is a bit extreme, yet not entirely without worth.

Protestants shy away from such concepts because of associations with 'monkish' abuses in Reformation history. However, as Christians already sanctified, and, yet, still undergoing the process of sanctification—a paradox, to be sure, but, nevertheless, Scriptural and true—there can be a place for these seemingly obscure acts of spiritual self-discipline. If we are actually recreated in the Holy Eucharist and through the hearing of the Word,

13. Wimmer, *Fasting in the New Testament*, 9.
14. Grothe, *Reclaiming Patterns of Pastoral Ministry*, 14.
15. Ibid.
16. Pelikan, *The Growth of Medieval Theology*, 127.
17. Pelikan, *The Illustrated Jesus Through the Centuries*, 150.

then repentance accompanied by fasting prepares us for this divine work. Although fasting, obviously, does not atone for sin, Christ may use it to prepare us for His work of forgiveness and reconciliation. And as our hearts of rock are recreated into His heart of flesh, we do experience His suffering love for those lost in this dark world.

Pastors fast, however, for less esoteric but equally valid reasons. If we are convinced that it is a good thing for some, it is a good thing for all. Yet how can pastors encourage others to do it, or appreciate it, if they themselves do not do it, or avoid it when it comes? Why would the laity embrace their suffering, when pastors negate their involuntary fasts? Bishop of Milan and one of the most influential doctors of the Church in the Fourth century, St. Ambrose in his instruction to priests, taught:

> Those who do not chastise their body and yet wish to preach to others are themselves considered castaways ... Paul did not consider it madness to chastise the body by fasting in order to make it subject to the Spirit. Thus, he says, "I chastise my body and bring it into subjection lest preaching to others, I myself should be found a castaway (1 Cor 9:27).[18]

Subjecting oneself to God in fasting helps the pastor to better lead the flock according to God's way and not ours. In the Epistle to the Galatians, St. Paul has us control the flesh in such a way that it will be subject to the Holy Ghost, since "walking by the Spirit means subduing the flesh and therefore living chastely".[19] As instruments of God, we are in a sense 'kept in tune' by ascetic practices like fasting, as our divine maestro plays His piece. We are directed according to His divine score. And seeking direction for the life of the congregation as her representative is a weightier responsibility than seeking direction for an individual's life and presents an even greater reason to fast.

Pastors, as representatives and fathers of the congregation, often require a 'special dose' of wisdom in the ministry of the Church and in the decisions concerning "practical" theology: applying the pure heavenly doctrine to impure worldly situations. St. Ambrose adds this:

> And what is the purpose of Scripture in teaching us that Peter fasted and that the mystery regarding the baptism of the Gentiles was revealed to him when he was fasting and praying (Acts 10:10), if not to show that the saints themselves, when they fast, become

18. Ambrose, *Letters*, 323.
19. AE 27:69.

more illustrious? Moses received the Law when he was fasting (Ex 34:28), and so Peter, when he was fasting, was taught the grace of the New Testament. Daniel too by virtue of his fasting, stopped the jaws of the lions and saw the events of future times (Dan 37:38; 9:2,3).[20]

It is undeniable that the Scriptures record some marvelous happenings while God's children fasted. We have already investigated how Christians have often received guidance by fasting. As captains of the ship and leaders of their congregations, pastors normally make the final decision on spiritual matters in their shepherding of the flock (in spite of the pressures that arise from the more democratic ecclesiastical processes in North America). For instance, in 2 Chronicles 20:3 we are told that all of Judah fasted including her leaders in order to ask for God's help before a battle. God graced them with advice in helping them make decisions in which God's will was not clear (i.e. either choice was amoral). Similarly, the Holy Spirit guides us today in our decision-making. St. Leo the Great, a bishop of Rome in the fifth century, counsels that we should "discipline the body to enable the spirit to receive direction from God"[21] just like the disciples fasted on their way to Antioch, as a way to seek God's counsel (Acts 13:2-3). Sometimes any decision may be permissible, and the best way is not clear. Fasting is a way of offering those important 'church life changing' decisions up to God.

Some mystics have argued that fasting causes "inner awakenings", an internal calm by slowing down the biological rhythm for self-assessment and personal searching.[22] This description is somewhat unsettling and may be better explained as something that helps us forget about our own ego and heightens our awareness of the needs and spiritual locality of others. How many committee meetings would run more peaceably when all those attending fasted before-hand, as a way of helping themselves view their brethren (and often 'enemies') through the eyes of the fasting Christ? David fasted for his enemies as recorded in Psalm 35:13 as a type of Christ. We see the same shining forth from our Lord's own words, "fast for those who persecute you" (Matt 5:44, 46 f), as He Himself did. David fasted while his enemies were sick. May we strive to pray more sincerely for our enemies and fast for them in the same Spirit. It may not change them, but it is sure to change us. By fasting, "our attitudes are transfigured, and we see oth-

---

20. Ambrose, *Letters*, 327.
21. Towns, *Fasting for Spiritual Breakthrough*, 1996.
22. Knobel, *Jewish Fasts*, 146.

ers through God's eyes, touch others with the wounded hands of Christ, encountering them as the suffering Jesus".[23]

Fasting may not change the enemy, but it will certainly change the faster, recreating his heart into a more resilient one: more apt to forgive. Fasting helps pastors to be those blessed peacemakers, as they are humbled and recreated into the servant, sensitive to those they are serving, so that the love of God, which alone can truly make peace, fills their ministry. Jesus' ministry embodied love in its purest form, and St. Paul, through apostolic imitation, continued to manifest it.[24] Imitat*ing* with a goal of being imitat*ed*, is a pastoral responsibility that comes along with the Divine Call to the Office of the Public Ministry:

> It is in light of this that *ecclesia* authorities have a responsibility to teach their people the nature and value of fasting so that they might help them to focus their minds effectively upon those things that are important to their humanity and happiness, to turn their entire being toward God, to consider how they stand with respect to their Creator . . . These matters are made difficult by the fallen state of humanity, wherein Christians are disordered in their loves, suffer disharmony within themselves and with the rest of creation, and are inclined specially to the lower concupiscible goods. In addition to this, all people are creatures of habit, habituated to family ways of thinking, acting, and feeling that are often not in conformity with those things required for their perfection and happiness.[25]

As spiritual warriors who fight to demolish the idols of the hearts, and all the demonic disordering that inevitably results in the descent of God and spiritual things as key priorities, pastors routinely fast for personal reasons as well. What the layman experiences in his Christian life is intensified in the life of the pastor. The attacks of the devil, exhibited in temptations of the flesh, are often worse for the pastor because of the consequential wide scope and impact of his sin on the believing community. Fasting, then, can be viewed as another tool that God has given to His shepherd to protect his sheep from every sort of wolf and danger. And when done in the right spirit, it is a privilege, a 'grace-full' way of serving his people, and mediating like a true priest. Such fasting is a way that the sheep, imitating the

---

23. Gillet, *The Jesus Prayer*, 90.
24. Grothe, *Reclaiming Patterns of Pastoral Ministry*, 67.
25. Loughlin, *Thomas Aquinas and the importance of fasting to the Christian life*, 355.

shepherd, can correspondingly care for him, since, as eloquently spoken by the Reformer in his *Devotional Writings*, the "fasting of others are my gain, the prayer of another pleads for me".[26]

And yet again, pastors do fast, even without choice. As pastors increasingly confront hurting situations, it becomes more and more natural to fast, to throw themselves at the feet of Almighty God, begging for His help and mercy, while simultaneously resting in the fact that our loving and compassionate Father does indeed help. It may take the form of prayers in which he cannot seem to cut short because he just can't stop agonizing over one of his sheep or a situation; or it may take the form of abstaining from food, and drink, because the suffering that he has endured on behalf of his flock has killed his natural appetite. Fasting is thus natural for the Christian. And whether we like it or not, it is good.

St. Paul praises its place in the Christian marriage, as he encourages husband and wife to pray and fast together (1 Cor 7:5) inspiring Tertullian while commenting on marriage and duty to call it a normal part of a Christian couple's life.[27] Today the same can be said about pastors since they are married to the Church as icons of the bridegroom. The pastor should fast for his flock and the flock should fast for her pastor. And naturally, if a pastor agrees with the Holy Scriptures and Christian tradition that fasting is important for lay people too, then, with love to sustain their faith, concern for their well-being, filled with divine jealousy for them, he should do what it takes to motivate his sheep to fast; namely, by doing it himself. The parishioners then see the proof, the fruits in the faster's life. They witness and imitate the changes in their pastor, so that the pastor, who likewise witnesses these changing patterns in his parishioners, can rejoice in the spiritual growth of this body of Christ (1 Thess 3:8).

Because of his high regard for the Holy Bible, St. Francis rightly revealed that there is very little in the Gospels on fasting and therefore unlike other orders, he did not oblige his friars to fast, but wanted them to be free to live under grace.[28] Pastors too should never be ordered to fast by their bishops or ecclesiastical supervisors. It is a gift that God has given to them. Instead, their love for the congregation and for God compels them to imitate Jesus[29] and, like St. Francis, live their lives as a continuous fast

---

26. AE 42:161.
27. Tertullian, *Treatise on Marriage and Remarriage*, 29. AE 28:14-15.
28. Sullivan, *Fast and Abstinence in the First order of St. Francis*, 6.
29. Ibid., 3.

manifesting their love for Christ.[30] As they model St. Paul and our Lord Jesus, their parishioners model them. May we never deprive each other of the lessons we learn in fasting. Picking up our crosses and following Jesus implies that Christians *do* fast: as the Body of Christ, in the unique cruciform shape that each Christian life manifests in all of its struggles and trials; and as spiritual warriors, from knees calloused by prayer and hearts injured by suffering. As both a broken Body and wounded warrior, the fasting Church remains strengthened by an indestructible faith incarnated in their unceasing and unconditional acts of love. Deliberate and intentional periods of fasting remind them and each other of these unseen realities. And though it may be immediately uncomfortable, the long-term value is priceless. As St. Ambrose summarizes:

> The hardship of fasting is compensated by tranquility of mind, it is lightened by practice, it is aided by leisure, nor beguiled by occupation; it is not burdened by the cares of the world, or occupied with others' troubles, or weighted down by the distractions of the city.[31]

It is already completed in Christ, who fasted for us, and fasts in and through us still.

---

30. Ibid., 1.
31. Ambrose, *Letters*, 351.

Appendix I

The True Fast (Isaiah 58:1-14):
a discussion of verses 3-7

Translation of Isaiah 58:3-7

v.3 WHY HAVE WE fasted and you have not seen it, we humbled/afflicted/made poor ourselves and you have not noticed? Behold on the day of your fast you pleasure/find delight/you do as you please and exploit/ oppress/ drive hard all your workers/toilers.

v.4 Behold you fast in quarrel/contention and strife and to strike with fist of wickedness. You cannot fast as you do today to make your voice to be heard on high.

v.5 Is this the kind of fast I choose, a day for a man to humble/afflict himself/his soul? To bow/bend his head like a reed/bulrush and lying in sackcloth and ashes? Is this what you call a fast and a day acceptable/favorable/pleasurable to the Lord God?

v.6 Is not *this* the fast I choose of him: to loose/open the chains/bonds of injustice/wickedness/ and to untie the cords/knots/bands of the yoke, to set the oppressed free and to break off every (kind of) yoke?

v.7 Is it not to share/divide your bread/food with the hungry and (cause to-*hif'il*) provide the poor/afflicted homeless/wanderers with shelter/house-when you see the naked, to clothe/cover him, and not to deny/hide/turn away (yourself=*hit'pael*) from your (own) flesh.

APPENDIX I

Introduction

Isaiah has often been referred to as the theologian of the Old Testament.[1] Although he was writing to the post-exilic Israelite community, addressing *their* immediate concerns, this St. Paul of the Old Testament was simultaneously addressing the immediate concerns of humanity in general: the need for a saviour.

The prophet Isaiah shares many characteristics with other Biblical prophets such as Amos, Hosea and Micah who were his contemporaries. Their subject matter contains a common theme: a message of social justice especially towards the poor and oppressed. And yet the message does not merely preach a kind of 'social Gospel', but like the other prophets—yet even more explicitly—Isaiah announces the coming Messiah.[2] For instance, throughout the book a repeated reference to "my servant" refers, of course, to the coming saviour, Jesus Christ.

Isaiah son of Amoz is often considered the greatest of the prophets or "forth-tellers". Beginning his ministry in 740 B.C., the year King Uzziah died, Isaiah spent most of his life in Jerusalem, displaying his greatest influence under King Hezekiah. Isaiah wrote during the expansion of the Assyrian Empire and the decline of Israel, while the spirits of God's people were low and burdened by their historic predicament. The message of the book completed around 700 BC is simply this: God will redeem his rebellious people from Babylon and that this restoration is like a new exodus.[3] This peace and safety are marks of the New Messianic age; shadows of the Christ who is the Redeemer.

The book is not only rich theologically, but full of literary treasure. The prose and poetry, though accurately documenting history, are aesthetically of unsurpassed beauty. By use of personification and allusions to earlier events in Israel's history, Isaiah offers the reader a unique glimpse into the Fatherly heart of our Lord and His gracious relationship with his rebellious children.

The literature can be broken up as follows: chapters 1-39 is a book of judgement against nations, and promise; chapters 40-66 is a book of comfort, specifically: (a) deliverance of Israel from sin; (b) the servant's ministry; and (c) everlasting deliverance and everlasting judgement. Section (c)

---

1. Hummel, *The Word Becoming Flesh*, 196.
2. Ibid., 157.
3. *Concordia Self Study Bible*, 1017.

which contains Isaiah 58 discusses: 1. comfort for the contrite and punishment for the wicked; 2. true worship versus false worship; and 3. sin, confession, and redemption.[4]

In short, we discover throughout the book the punishment and redemption dynamic paving the way to the cross of Christ. Even though the first 39 chapters mainly concern judgement of sin, preparing the path for the last 27 chapters which are mainly concerned with the hope, comfort and promise of Messiah, we see waves of Law and Gospel within chapters and even verses. Chapters 56-66, which contain our text, are not just predictions but are "sustained projections of the prophet's Law-Gospel vision into the future, the precise message bringing comfort and promise to the exiles".[5] Although Isaiah predicts Cyrus as an instrument of God for delivering Israel from Babylonians, at the same time he predicts Christ delivering His people from the devil. Appropriately then the name Isaiah, "the Lord Saves", summarizes the central message of a book which Luther describes as "truly full of living, comforting, tender sayings for all poor consciences and miserable, disturbed hearts".[6]

Isaiah 58 addresses the specific abuses that retarded the recovery of post-exilic Israel.[7] The prophet who exposed the empty ritual of God's people in chapter 1, discusses here specifically one religious activity: fasting. The message is that no external piety, but only true righteousness will please God and thereby change their situation.[8] Throughout the text, God addresses the Israelites as a group, in second person plural (except in the third sentence of verse 5, which is singular, indicating that God is addressing the speaker/representative of this group). The "trumpet call" in verse 1, used to summon people to a holy war or announce the beginning of a solemn day of worship or fasting, is meant to rouse this group of hearers[9] to action concerning their false worship.[10] If they begin doing this (spoken in the imperfect tense), then God's light will swiftly break forth (v.8f). And so we hear not only the complaint of the hypocritical worshipper (a complaint

---

4. *Concordia Self Study Bible*, 1018.
5. Hummel, *The Word Becoming Flesh*, 185.
6. AE 35:278.
7. Leupold, *Exposition of Isaiah II*, 283.
8. Ibid.
9. Delitzsch, *The Prophecies of Isaiah III*, 389-391.
10. Herbert, *Isaiah 40-66*, 145.

APPENDIX I

often echoing our own), but also the reply of God almighty in both Law and Gospel terms.[11]

Although Isaiah 58 is not a characteristic prophecy but more of an admonition, speaking as a teacher and instructor, it still has the prophetic character rebuking the sin and proclaiming the promise;[12] articulating in prose the underlying theme of the entire Scriptures. Therefore, though this segment of the text contains mainly Law, the promises of God are unveiled in the verses that follow which extrapolate God's gifts to us: the love of God, His healing power and illuminating light; His righteousness which clears the way; and His listening to prayer to every appeal and cry for help. If the Israelites change their way, their fasting will bring about much more than merely one answered prayer, but multiplied blessings. Jehovah loves to shower gifts upon His children!

Due to perceived incongruities in theme, style, content, and language in Isaiah, particularly in the relationship between the first and second halves of the book, higher critics call the author of the text here presented "II Isaiah" or "Deutero-Isaiah" (and Isa III is referred to as "Trito-Isaiah" with the transition happening somewhere in chapter 56) demonstrating their difficulty with the authorship of the book. Orthodox scholars make a *literary* distinction within the book, recognizing that these differences are nothing more than our prophet writing in different historical contexts at different points in his life (i.e. hence we distinguish between 'late' and 'early' Isaiah), and that the poem is in fact somewhat of an anthology consisting of diverse materials.[13] The underlying theme remains united and pointed: the repetition of "Holy One of Israel" continually brings us back to the message of salvation. Where the higher critics divide the book according to three authors, we understand the text to reflect three shifts in the prophet's vision. For instance, a conservative exegete treats this segment in Isaiah 58 as a third shift in Isaiah's own vision as he "corrects possible enthusiastic misunderstandings of his own eschatological exuberance".[14]

Concerning Isaiah 58, higher critics point out one particularity attempting to discredit unity in text and authorship. Verses 13-14 discuss behaviour on the Sabbath, a grouping which, at first glance, appears misplaced. Yet, on further investigation, this 'palindrome' fits neatly in with

11. Young, *The Book of Isaiah*, 417.
12. Leupold, *Exposition of Isaiah II*, 283.
13. Hummel, *The Word Becoming Flesh*, 184, 194.
14. Ibid., 225.

APPENDIX I

the theme of "true fasting" or better yet, "true worship", since fasting and Sabbath observance were not mutually exclusive events. The association of the Sabbath with "self-mortification" in Leviticus 16:31, a likely synonym for fasting, may account for the inclusion of verses 13-14 in this chapter, which otherwise seem to be unrelated.[15] Furthermore when we look at the one God-ordained fast recorded in Leviticus 16:29,31;23:27-32, occurring on the Day of Atonement, the connection with the Sabbath becomes clear. One should not work on God's holy day, whether it be a fast or a Sabbath or (most likely) both (Lev 16:31), and yet business was rampant amongst the Israelites during these holy days. Nor was the faster permitted to make *others* (i.e. his employees) work on that day either, another violation addressed in verse 3. The Sabbath was a time to express love for God and receive His gift of rest, who then sends his people forth to fast, as an opportunity to show love to his neighbour.[16] The two activities worked hand in hand.

COMMENTARY

verse 3

The Israelites that Isaiah is addressing had forgotten the true meaning and purpose of fasting. Because they were relatively prosperous, they believed themselves to be on good terms with God. Believing that they lacked sin, the fast became another avenue of Israelite hypocrisy: oppression of the poor and helpless by the rich expressing their forgetfulness of how poor they once were and blindness as to how poor they still are.[17] Done properly, with the right spirit and right attitude, *this* day could have potentially been a good day for a fast since the returning exiles had been liberated as their prophet (Isa 40-55) had declared; yet it was into a condition of poverty and hardship. Instead of humbly and honestly seeking God's help and pity, they made a mockery of Him.[18]

It is interesting that there are no references to regularly appointed fast days amongst the Israelites until after the exile (Zech 7:1-14; 8:18f), although under a threat of invasion from the Babylonian army a fast had

---

15. Herbert, *Isaiah 40-66*, 144.
16. Ibid.
17. McKenzie, *Second Isaiah*, 166.
18. Herbert, *Isaiah 40-66*, 145.

APPENDIX I

been proclaimed (Jer 36:9).[19] The one mandatory fast day was the Day of Atonement (of particular interest to the Christian since this day, one of the most important in the Jewish calendar, most explicitly pointed to Christ, the 'One who atones'). Those who violated this command on this great day of national repentance (10th of *Tishri*) were punishable by death.[20] There are several other instances where Israel fasted (e.g. 1 Sam 7:6, Judges 20:26, I Kings 21:12, to name a few) but these were all self imposed, later appointments. These special fasts were connected to outstanding days of divine judgement commemorated by the nation, specifically marking the commandment and siege of Jerusalem, and the capture, destruction and murder of Gedalliah (Zech 7:3, 8:18-19; 7:1-16). Because they often functioned exclusively as signs of sorrow,[21] the prophet Zechariah in 7:1-16 questions the validity of these fasts that were often a source of great perplexity. After the restoration of the temple there is a question as to whether or not they should continue.[22] *This* is the fasting that the exiles boast about but is actually heartless and a 'dead work' and therefore worthless in God's sight.[23]1

Many Israelites saw their fasting as a formulaic way of "getting something" out of God instead of as an activity flowing out of a repentant and burdened heart. They trusted in their own pious ascetic works instead of God[24] who they then questioned as to whether He was living up to His part of the covenant.[25] In verses 1-2, we are told that these Israelites thought they were a pious and holy group, in good standing with the Lord God, and so they found "pleasure in drawing near to God". Behaving like they were on good terms with God[26] and feeling they had the right to demand of God,

---

19. Ibid., 144.
20. Kittel, *The Theological Dictionary of the New Testament*, 927.
21. Leupold, *Exposition of Isaiah II*, 285
22. Westerman, *Isaiah 40-66*, 335.
23. Delitzsch, *The Prophecies of Isaiah III*, 385. In the post-exilic period, the number of annual public fasts increased (Ezra 8:21-21, Neh 9:1). These fasts owe their origin to customs established during Exile, though in later Jewish tradition they were given a wider historical rationale. Later the Purim fast was also added to them. Zachariah urges that they be continued on the understandings that they are "seasons of joy and gladness" and not seasons of sorrow, now that the Temple has been rebuilt. (Freedman, *Isaiah II*, 774)
24. Young, *The Book of Isaiah*, 417
25. Buttrick, *The Book of Isaiah*, 679
26. Leupold, *Exposition of Isaiah II*, 285.

their demands were based on their perceived good works and religiosity.[27] They approach God daily expecting Him to act in their favour, ignorant of their sin.[28] These words of the "work-righteous" who hold up their fasting before God and complain that He takes no notice,[29] have indeed been heard by God. God has 'seen' and does 'know,' but He is certainly not impressed.

In their eyes, fasting was supposed to be of some worth and merit. Yet *this* fasting, even as a perceived 'good work', was not much of one; it wasn't that great even according to *their own* standards. The hardships of their fast were merely 'minor inconveniences' and did not reflect a repentant attitude. In the preceding verses we see that people carried on in their normal selfish and worldly manner, "prevented from the divine worship and absorption in the spiritual character of the day to the most thoroughly selfish purposes".[30] They focussed on simple external rites ignoring the central point that "the fast serves to demonstrate the seriousness and earnestness and intensity of their prayer for deliverance".[31] What did a little abstinence matter if they could retain their basic life style of disobedience and still get God to act for them? Further, they made the fast easier by idleness and made up for lost time by getting their laborers to work all the harder. A fast implied universal cessation from labour, yet these men made it a class affair, for 'employers only'![32] Yet God cannot be fooled or bought. It is as if God says, jumping ahead to verse 5: "You fast for one day, *'Big Deal'*!"

The verb tense contrasts the people's perspective versus God's. Throughout the text it is worth noting that where man seems to speak in the perfect tense, God speaks in the imperfect tense.[33] The people are talking about *this* particular fast asking, "where are the results of *this* fast in which we have caused intense infliction upon ourselves (the *pi'el* is used)?" Yet God refers to the bigger picture, making statements about *all* their fasts in general. "In *all* your fasts this happens . . . " To reinforce this idea, we notice that in verse 6, when God outlines the type of fast He has indeed chosen,

---

27. Ibid., 284.
28. Delitzsch, *The Prophecies of Isaiah III*, 385.
29. Ibid., 385.
30. Ibid., 386.
31. Westerman, *Isaiah 40-66*, 336.
32. Buttrick, *The Book of Isaiah*, 679.
33. There is, however, one exception. God uses the perfect tense in verse 7: "to cover him".

APPENDIX I

"*Tzom*" has no definite article, and follows a verb with relative force[34] indicating the *general nature* of the fast He chooses. Furthermore, throughout the passages, Isaiah emphasizes the *kind of fast* and not the kind of faster, grammatically isolating the fast from the faster, insinuating the absoluteness of the terms, that this is not just the kind of fast God has chosen for the Israelites, but is the kind of Fast (in absolute terms), that our Father desires and pleasures in; a fast in which He sees His children all getting along.

תִּמְצְאוּ־חֵפֶץ the idea of *their pleasuring* in the Hebrew is not an easy one to understand[35] but given the context, appears to address the 'business practice' of these people. They carried on their business in a typical sinful manner as if this day was not at all special. They did as they pleased and desired to fulfill their own interests in contrast with what God pleasures and desires. This fast day, this Sabbath even, was not practiced with God in mind, but was absorbed with the thoughts of men. "You pursue your own business" (which is your pleasure!) and "oppress your workers", or better, "you press your occupations" (i.e. occupy yourself with business affairs). In Deuteronomy 15:2, the noun is applied to the oppression of a debtor. But here it refers to those who owe *labour*, or obligations to labour, one who "eats the bread of toil" (Ps 127:2).[36] This clever pleasure/delight motif outlines in general what pleases God versus man. This general idea is then flushed out in concrete terms in verse 4.[37]

You "drive hard all your workers" or "drive on their toilers", the root of the verb is the Amharic title of the king of Ethiopia, 'Negus', and the root is used of the oppression of Israel in Egypt.[38] The verb carries overtones of slave-driving, especially in context of these Egyptian oppressors (Ex 3:7).[39] These Israelites who were once oppressed have now become the oppressors, and now face God's judgement: the "day" of fast in verses 3-9 simultaneously referring to the "day" of God's judgement; a pun used later in Mark 2:20 when "they will fast on that day".[40]

---

34. Young, *The Book of Isaiah vol III*, 419.
35. Delitzsch, *The Prophecies of Isaiah III*, 386.
36. Ibid., 386.
37. Buttrick, *The Book of Isaiah*, 679.
38. Young, *The Book of Isaiah vol III*, 417.
39. Herbert, *Isaiah 40-66*, 146.
40. Freedman, *Isaiah II*, 774.

verse 4

A glaring contrast between their conduct and the point of the fast which is to enable them to draw near with importunate prayer to God who is enthroned on high is revealed.[41] Instead, "Behold" this is what their fasting results in, not God's blessing but in even more sin (i.e. fighting and quarreling). The NIV translates the first phrase as, "ends with quarrel". Yet this is misleading. The fast is *characterized* by quarrelling. It is also characterized by strife and contention, instead of by preparation of mind for prayer.[42] These people cannot carry on their fast in this hypocritical manner and expect God to hear their prayer; "to make their voice audible on high".[43] The chiastic arrangement in the negative voice reinforces this idea: Israel does not engage in this practice so that their voice may be heard on high, for if they did so, their entire approach to fasting would be different.[44]

This sort of fasting which is undertaken as a duty and method of manipulating the divine, instead of as an expression of faith, can produce an edgy, irritable community, especially in difficult climactic conditions. Thus, fasting made these people twice more irritable than they normally were.[45] The use of the *hif'il*, that "*they cause to strike* others" is worth noting.[46] In fasting, these Israelites afflict *themselves* and then afflict *others*. Because their fasting is not motivated by love, the affliction they experience, in a sense, *causes* them to afflict others! The suggestion by St. Augustine that abstaining from "strife and discord" is a true fast[47] is already found in this negative definition of what a true fast *is not,* suggesting rather that it is the opposite. Similarly, the ancients said, "not eating is a *natural* fast; abstaining from sin is a *spiritual* fast".[48]

Some however argue that the wrangling and quarreling is to be interpreted not as a result of fasting, but ought to be understood as connected

---

41. Delitzsch, *The Prophecies of Isaiah III*, 385-386.
42. Young, *The Book of Isaiah vol III*, 418.
43. Leupold, *Exposition of Isaiah II*, 286.
44. Young, *The Book of Isaiah vol III*, 418.
45. Delitzsch, *The Prophecies of Isaiah III*, 386.
46. The bare idea of the root verb of the infinitive construct... refers to the general character of the act without the specification of person, gender and number (Kelley, *Biblical Hebrew*, 434). A *particular* incident is not here being referred. Instead, the "striking" in general which characterizes these fasts, is highlighted.
47. Augustine, *Sermons on Liturgical Seasons*, 85.
48. Delitzsch, *The Prophecies of Isaiah III*, 387.

APPENDIX I

to the methods of their business affairs,[49] reminiscent of the present-day market place environment in the region. This is sensical if the fasting they underwent really wasn't all that difficult and involving in the first place.

verse 5

"Is this" points *backwards* to the kind of fast with which God is not impressed. Isaiah continues to flush out the details of the sort of fast that may satisfy man, but not God.

God speaks in the interrogative for emphasis, exhibiting his humanlike emotions (i.e. functioning as anthropopathic) as He dialogues with man, similar to a father dialoguing with a child. So, it has been said this poem is a dialogue between *Yahweh* and Israelites.[50] We can almost empathize with God's saddened heart as He scolds His people out of love. God says sarcastically, "will you call *this* a fast?" At no point is the reader tempted to answer "yes" to His rhetorical questioning.[51]

A "straight rush" is an example of satire in Isaiah,[52] since it is easily bent, and thus furnishes a suitable figure for a bent-over worshipper.[53] Consistent with this criticism of the hypocritical faster, Jesus said on Sermon on Mount that the Pharisees "make their face look dismal".[54]

A more descriptive and informative translation for "lying in sackcloth and ashes (or "caused to lie down"; *hif'il*) would be "spreading sackcloth and ashes under him" (NRSV). This special demonstration of discomfort by making a bed for one's self in sackcloth and ashes,[55] is nothing more than outward show meriting human recognition (as in Zechariah 7:5-6, they fasted for themselves and not for God in a spirit contrary to that encouraged in Matt 6:17-18: to fast so others won't know you are). Yet 'is this the kind of fast that inflict man's soul in truth? A day acceptable to Jehovah?'[56] One could paraphrase the idea of the verse as follows: "can *such things as these pass* for a fast that I have pleasure in, as a day for a man to afflict his

49. Westerman, 1968, 335.
50. Mckenzie, *Second Isaiah*, 165.
51. Leupold, *Exposition of Isaiah II*, 287.
52. Buttrick, *The Book of Isaiah*, 680.
53. Young, *The Book of Isaiah vol III*, 419.
54. Leupold, *Exposition of Isaiah II*, 286.
55. Ibid., 286.
56. Delitzsch, *The Prophecies of Isaiah III*, 387.

APPENDIX I

soul, to bow down his head like a bulrush and spread sackcloth and ashes under him, *is this what you call a fast acceptable* for Jehovah?"

The NIV translates the first phrase: "Is it *only* for . . . " which I believe to be a poor modern translation as it suggests that this outward show is a condition for fasting, but that the fasting that God desires requires so much more. Yet the text indicates that God is not at all impressed with this outward show; He rejects their fasting in full. Another poor translation, in my opinion, is found in the NASB which replaces the last conjunction "and" with "even". In contemporary English the phrase could possibly be understood to mean that these people have not only failed to fulfill the requirements of a normal fast but have not *even* fulfilled God's [lower] standards.

verse 6

Now the prophet explains the sort of fast that does pleasure God, by sketching a brief ideal picture of a community in which the needs of one are supplied by the excesses of others.[57] "This" points *forward* to the fast God will describe as desirable and true.[58] Notice how God answers His own question[59] as guilty man stands in silence; *He* outlines what is proper, effectual fasting. God chooses/determines what a true fast is because He is our superior and He knows best. True fasting is not merely fasting but is fasting coupled with showing mercy to brethren.[60] As mentioned above, fasting was understood to be intermingled with petitionary prayer (and also petitionary prayer for forgiveness, which is why repentance was also closely related). Well, now, God explains how fasting is inseparable from the act of showing mercy to others. Incidentally, the early Church understood the fast as an activity done together with prayer and almsgiving.

The use of the infinitive absolute in this verse, serving to strengthen, reinforce and intensify the verbal idea, with an emphasis on its duration and continuation,[61] implies that the three prescriptive activities explicitly stated in this verse ("loosening the bonds", "untying the bands", and "setting the oppressed free") are not only related in character but are to be *ongo-*

---

57. Incidentally, this segment may be the original sketch for Matthew 25:31-46 (McKenzie, *Second Isaiah*, 166).
58. Delitzsch, *The Prophecies of Isaiah III*, 388.
59. Westermann, *Isaiah 40-66*, 323.
60. Delitzsch, *The Prophecies of Isaiah III*, 387.
61. Kelley, *Biblical Hebrew*, 185.

ing and are not one-time actions. Some translations state "Is not this the fast *I have* chosen" which is an acceptable translation grammatically but may suggest that God has chosen this fast in past time for a certain people, instead of pressing the teaching that God's choice remains the same for all people. He would have his children 'fast' like this all the time. Thus, the three infinitives demonstrate the "permanence of divine requirements", while the imperfect which concludes the sentence lends "variety and life to the mode of expression".[62]

The use of the *pi'el*, consistent with this function of the infinitive-absolute, indicates the intensity/seriousness of the verbal action of "opening the bonds" and "setting free the oppressed" which are quick, simple, and intentional actions (the *hif'il* for "loosening the yoke", emphasizes the intentional action of causing the yoke to be loosened so that the enslaved can slip away).

In verses 6-7 all four verbs express the idea of *liberation*. The metaphors deserve attention: "to loose the bonds of wicked" i.e. oppressive practices such as the harsh treatment of debtors; "to undo the thongs of the yoke", i.e. to lift the burdensome exactions; "to let the oppressed go free", i.e. to liberate the bankrupt whose families might be sold into slavery (Neh 5:5). During the Chaldean siege of Jerusalem slaves of 'Israelitish' descent were declared emancipated, doubtless to gain divine favor; but when the Chaldeans withdrew, their masters claimed them again (Jer 34: 18-22).[63] God is here revealing Israel's sin of gross violation of the command to release Israel's slaves every three years as stated in Jeremiah 34:8-22[64] and also indirectly rebuking them for repeating the same despotic disposition which they themselves underwent.[65] The "homeless poor" refers to vagrants and political refugees, of whom a troubled time produces a vast number.[66] These fasters were often the ones responsible for imprisonment of these poor[67] and therefore had the power and authority to release them.

This revolutionary-like imagery, often hailed by defenders of Social Gospel theology, reminds us less of *our* works and more of *God's* work. We recall the *Christus Victor* motif, when we remember that Christ descended

62. Young, *The Book of Isaiah*, 419.
63. Buttrick, *The Book of Isaiah*, 680-681.
64. Young, *The Book of Isaiah*, 419.
65. Delitzsch, *The Prophecies of Isaiah III*, 388.
66. Buttrick, *The Book of Isaiah*, 680-681.
67. Leupold, *Exposition of Isaiah II*, 287.

into Hell to set the prisoners free in a warrior-like manner. So, too, the exodus from Egypt mirrors that event when the Israelites were set free by the living God. "Bondage" was a powerful word-image for these former slaves, and so it was considered to be a heroic and philanthropic act to "loosen bonds", bonds with which they were all too familiar, and to declare liberty.[68] Similarly the "ones being oppressed" is a strong synonym for those who are cruelly, unjustly, forcibly oppressed, as were the Israelites under the Egyptians. In short, God advises the Israelites to liberate others, as God has liberated them, as God liberates all of us in Christ crucified, through the waters of Holy Baptism, from the oppression of all of our current enslaving situations.

This, then, is the *true* fast: having a new attitude, looking to help others, and mirroring the heart of God.[69] His love moves us to see His face in other people, and hence love them, exhibited in acts of helping and freeing of "the least of these". True fasting is less about self-denial and more about loving sacrifice through self-humbling. The passage suggests that if these people want mercy from God, they should first *show* mercy to others.[70] True fasting is not a material achievement performed to one's own advantage, following Jeremiah's protest (Jer 14:12) against the violence found amongst the "sham holiness" of external observance, but rather true fasting is the *real* "bowing of soul" (v. 5) in moral action.[71]

verse 7

The prophet in verse 6 lifts his voice like a trumpet in judgement against his fellow worshipers.[72] Yet here in verse 7 it is counteracted with hints of the Gospel, when we reflect upon how God acted in a true-fast-like-fashion in Jesus Christ, towards us, even though we acted as His oppressors. Christ delivered us from bondage in baptism and fed/feeds us hungry, poor sinners in the Eucharist, providing us with the shelter of His home, the Church.

The verse encourages the fasting Israelites to provide for these needy people by denying themselves something: that is *God's* kind of fasting. As other manuscripts suggest, a better translation for the second phrase is "to

68. Westerman, *Isaiah 40-66*, 337.
69. Young, *The Book of Isaiah vol III*, 420.
70. Leupold, *Exposition of Isaiah II*, 287.
71. Kittel, *The Theological Dictionary of the New Testament*, 928.
72. Buttrick, *The Book of Isaiah*, 681.

bring the homeless into *your* house" which is asking more than merely providing them with a home. It asks you to give up some of your own privacy; not only giving bread but sharing some of your own, going half hungry yourself. When people fast in love for each other, for "the least of these", then God will answer their prayer, and a more complete restoration for Israel will result.[73] Similarly, one possible paraphrase connecting the third phrase to the first two reads: "the afflicted, even refugees, are to be provided with the shelter of one's own home; likewise cover the naked".[74] This puts an entirely new spin on the Hebrew for "humbling/afflicting/making oneself poor". God's kind of fast would have His people afflict themselves, make themselves *poor for the sake of the other*, as an expression of Christian love, as opposed to the superficial ritual of the Pharisees whose, as likened by George Eliot in *Middlemarch*, "celestial intimacies seemed not to improve their domestic manners".[75]

The NIV translates the last phrase "flesh and blood" which suggests that one ought act this way only to family relations or those of the same ethnicity and not to strangers. Yet the "wanderer" (wanderer or homeless is the variant reading in the Septuagint and occurs only once in the Hebraic Scriptures) refers not only to Israelite men, but the persecuted in general.[76] It speaks against those who refuse to act humanely (*hit'pael* imperfect is reflexive: "do it to yourself", by your own will, "turn self from"), since "flesh" most likely refers to all of humankind,[77] in the spirit of the Good Samaritan, constituting "the indivisible united and a brotherhood pledged to mutual love".[78]

Central Thought

Fasting for God means fasting for others; giving up of ourselves for the sake of someone else (and so we remember that Christ fasted for us not merely during His temptation in the desert but in all His works and in His very being). The false fasting or self-*affliction* of the Israelites resulted in the *affliction* of others and the neglect of the afflicted.

73. Leupold, *Exposition of Isaiah II*, 288.
74. Young, *The Book of Isaiah vol III*, 420.
75. Buttrick, *The Book of Isaiah*, 679.
76. Delitzsch, *The Prophecies of Isaiah III*, 388.
77. Young, *The Book of Isaiah vol III*, 420.
78. Buttrick, *The Book of Isaiah*, 681.

Appendix II

*Fasting in the Presence of God:
an Exegetical Study of Matthew 9:14-17*

Translation

14 Then the disciples of John approached him saying, "why do we and the Pharisees fast, but your disciples do not fast?" 15 And Jesus said to them, "Can the wedding guests mourn as long as the bridegroom is with them? The days will come, when the bridegroom is taken away from them, and they will fail to fast. 16 And not one puts/sews a piece of new/unshrunk cloth on an old garment, for the patch tears away from the garment and a worse tear is made. 17 Neither is new wine put into old wineskins; if it is, the skins burst and the wine is spilled/pours out, and the wineskins are destroyed/ruined/perish; but the new wine is put into fresh wineskins, and so both are preserved.

Introduction

The ancient Church believed St. Matthew to be the earliest of the Gospels (perhaps as early as 42 AD) and held the disciple Matthew the tax collector as its author.[1] Because of Matthew's background, his Gospel has often been regarded as the most 'Jewish' of all the Gospels (i.e., expressed in Jewish

---

1. Franzmann, *Follow me: Discipleship according to St. Matthew*, 178.

APPENDIX II

terminology, language, allusions, and metaphors). Yet the Gospel was written for and embraced by others as well.

It is imperative in understanding the Gospel according to St. Matthew that the reader recognize its didactic character. Matthew gives the fullest account of the creation of Jesus' disciples: how they were called, trained, etc.[2] As God is known by His works, so the Christ becomes known to men by His disciples, by the men whom He called and molded in His own image.[3] The teaching is passed from Christ to the disciples to us. Matthew as a disciple aims to teach the intimate relationship between Christ and all who hear His word[4] and is hence truly a "gift of God" to us, as the name "Matthew" translates.

Accordingly, Matthew uses various tools in achieving his goal. He designed and structured his Gospel for it to be easily remembered. For instance, the words and deeds of Christ are organized topically and not chronologically.[5] The use of contrast is a common teaching tool.[6] What is the content of the teaching? Namely, that Jesus Christ is the Messiah, the one for whom the Jews eagerly awaited. Matthew demonstrates this truth and generates a response in the hearer/reader through a variety of themes and literary means: (1) emphasizing the demand of Christ for repentance of the whole man; (2) asserting that the way to obedience is by faith alone since only God is good, severely rebuking the Scribes and Pharisees who trust in themselves; (3) conveying material continuous with Old Testament images and background; and (4) presenting Christ in a sober, colourless and quiet way in His work, letting the facts speak for themselves.[7]

The passage in discussion exhibits some of these traits. Yet one of Matthew's most helpful devices in understanding our text is his positioning of it in the greater structural context. Matthew 9:14-17 is preceded by the calling of Matthew the sinner and Jesus' table fellowship with him. Thus, the question of fasting follows naturally from this incident. Jesus' radical actions always raise crucial questions regarding His authority and identity. The healing of the ruler's dead daughter follows our text, exhibiting how Christ's teaching and words are always qualified with action.

2. Ibid, 174.
3. Franzmann, *The Word of the Lord Grows*, 174.
4. Ibid., 172.
5. Ibid., 171.
6. Ibid., 173.
7. Ibid., 180-181.

APPENDIX II

Matthew is careful in selecting his players. Recognizing the significance of the ones raising the question about fasting is of crucial importance in interpreting the text. Jesus is questioned about His disciples' unconventional behaviour by the disciples of John the Baptist who had not yet grasped the meaning of this man Jesus in their midst. Although the imprisoned John knew who Jesus was (i.e., the lamb of God), his disciples were left with little guidance. Jesus uses their inquiry to assert His authority and identity.

Scholars however are divided regarding the motivation of the question posed to Jesus. Were these disciples friendly or hostile to Christ? Previously, there was a hostile questioning of Jesus' piety by the Scribes, and then by the Pharisees and now the disciples of John are recorded as questioning Him. Following in the footsteps of their leader, John's disciples probably fasted a lot, at least twice a week,[8] and were probably fasting along with the Pharisees during Jesus' feast at Matthew's house. It is likely that John's disciples had not yet understood the meaning of Jesus and the role of their leader in the economy of salvation, and now, in His absence, are at best confused and at worst, bitter (Mark has John's disciples teamed up with the Pharisees during the confrontation, implying that they were in fact hostile to Christ). Because these loyal disciples of John and faithful imitators of his pious lifestyle are not in a position to be corrected or directed by John, who is imprisoned, Jesus is left to defend Himself amongst a people who may not hold His opinion in high regard. Almost always at issue with the Jews is the correct interpretation of, or the proper adherence to, the Mosaic law of the Pharisaic tradition of the elders.[9] Because they see Christ as a fraud, they attempt to debunk His teachings and His disciples with whom He shares authority and who are enemies of Jerusalem by association.[10] John's disciples may have been amongst this antagonistic group.

Yet others have argued that the questioning was not so much one of hostility, but perplexity in this matter,[11] that in fact the disciples did not like the Pharisees and thirsted for enlightenment. Thus, it is argued, that they were not accusing Jesus but honestly inquiring. For all practical purposes,

---

8. France, *Matthew*, 168.

9. Kingsbury, *Matthew as Story*, 65.

10. God's enemies cannot be satisfied. John came fasting and they said he had a demon. Jesus comes eating and drinking and they call Him a glutton (Matt 11:18-19).

11. Lenski, *Interpretation of St. Matthew's Gospel*, 367.

APPENDIX II

the issue can remain unresolved since the question is much less important than the answer.

> Because Jesus' ministry of teaching, preaching, and healing is a proffering of salvation to Israel, the element of conflict does not dominate the plot of Matthew's story.[12]

Furthermore, the innocence and righteousness *of Jesus* is constantly maintained by Matthew. We should accordingly keep the discourse focused on Jesus and not the other players. In the narrative, no person or event displaces the person or authority of Jesus of Nazareth as Messiah and the relationship of this message to the Gospel. All aspects of our text point to Christ. For instance,

> The implied reader is led to sense a tension between Jesus and Jewish leaders, yet this conflict is carefully orchestrated so that Jesus is not directly attacked for something he himself does.[13]

The discussion is about the meaning of this man Jesus. When all is said and done, Matthew leaves no room for doubts regarding Christ's divinity. For example, John encouraged his disciples to fast. Yet Jesus does not contradict the Law by not having His disciples fast since the Law prescribed only one mandatory fast day and the rest were considered voluntary.[14] Matthew upholds Jesus as the fulfiller, not destroyer, of the Law even though He is above the Law. Matthew is careful in keeping the focus of the text on the teaching of Jesus concerning His authority as God and identity as the Messiah and offends the Jews only where necessary.

Matthew accomplishes his goal by teaching two interrelated things: 1. He discusses the proper place of the Law in the dawning Messianic age; and 2. He warns that because Jesus is the Messiah, and His work is to die, the time of joy is temporary.[15]

verse 14

Fasting played an important role in the piety of Judaism, especially in Pharisaism: it acted as a sign of devotion and religion; it was intimately

---

12. Kingsbury, *Matthew as Story*, 58.
13. Ibid.
14. Lenski, *Interpretation of St. Matthew's Gospel*, 368.
15. Albright, *Matthew*, 108.

related with almsgiving/showing mercy and prayer [which is why Luke connects fasting and the offering prayers (Luke 5:33)]; it was a means of seeking guidance from the Lord; and it was often attached to repentance and mourning. Although there was only one mandatory fast on the Day of Atonement, other voluntary fasts existed, and fasting was encouraged. John the Baptist was respected because of his strict piety which included fasting (Mat 11:18). So, too, his disciples, along with the Pharisees, fasted often. An early insertion of the Latin text of verse 14 reads fasting 'often' or 'frequently' which would be characteristic of Jewish piety of the day. Religious Jews fasted; especially teachers. It would have been troubling for John's disciples to witness this Jewish teacher Jesus (who was known to be a teacher above other teachers and a prophet) and His disciples abstaining from a fast when everyone else was fasting, and instead 'feasting' by eating with sinners (as recorded in verse 10). Normal teachers fasted. Yet Jesus was not an ordinary teacher.

John's disciples' confusion is understandable as the question really boiled down to "why does one who preaches repentance not display acts of repentance?"[16] It demonstrates the disciples' lack of clarity concerning Jesus and His relationship with John. The question opens the door for the revelation of an entirely new teaching accompanying this new Messianic epoch in Jewish history. John's asceticism is about to be contrasted with Jesus' celebration: John announces sombre repentance whereas Jesus announces good news and celebration.[17] John's reform movement was possibly understood by some disciples to repair the old order, by penitence and fasting, by "shrinking the patch" (jumping ahead to the following image); whereas a more flexible dispensation was needed (i.e. new wineskins) in order to accommodate the eschatological joy of the dawning kingdom.[18]

verse 15

Jesus answers them with a striking analogy of a bridegroom and bride. It is striking because of the implications that the image of bridegroom had in Jewish theology.[19] "Bridegroom" is a later Old Testament title for God as the

16. Davies, *St. Matthew*, 107.
17. Ibid, 109.
18. Freedman, *Isaiah II*, 776.
19. Although it is possible that this saying has nothing to do with the bridegroom/Messiah allegory at all, but that the choice of the metaphor is simply due to the common

husband of Israel (Isa 62:5). In the exodus, Israel was married to God in the covenant. After Israel broke that bond, a future marriage was promised[20] (a marriage that happens in our baptism). Jesus is that promise fulfilled! Jesus is the bridegroom of His disciples who are the new Israel.[21] By referring to Himself as "the bridegroom" Jesus was once again ascribing to Himself what the Old Testament had ascribed to the Lord. He was interpreting His ministry in terms of the covenant of fidelity, love, and the forgiving patience of the Lord which the Old Testament had summed up in the figure of the husband (Isa 54: 5,7,8; Jer 62:5; Isa 62:5, 49:18; Song of Songs depicts God as the husband-lover of His bride).[22]

Accordingly, the New Testament speaks about *the Church* as the bride and Christ as the bridegroom in a variety of places. Jesus' own analogies are congruent with the notion. He says that the Kingdom of God is like a wedding feast of a king (Matt 22:2). The Father is the king. Yet Christ alludes that He Himself is also the King (whose kingdom is not of this world) asserting the unity of His personhood with the Father [also μετ' αὐτῶν: "with them" comes forward to emphasize that Jesus is Immanuel, "God with us" (1:23)]. Another instance of this motif occurs in Matthew 25 in which the kingdom of heaven is described as a gathering of virgins meeting the bridegroom with oil in their lamps. Christ as bridegroom is a common theme. The Revelation to St. John uses this imagery as well. The bride is considered the heavenly Jerusalem, and the wedding feast is often connected to the messianic banquet occurring in Jesus' table fellowship with sinners which pinnacles in the Lord's Supper.

"Wedding guests" may be better understood as "sons of the bridechamber" or "children" and is not akin to our modern depictions of a wedding. Jesus is not talking about all the guests, but rather about a selected few who would help with the wedding arrangements.

> The closest friends of the married couple were called children of the bridechamber and would partake in all the festivities of the week with the couple since the honeymoon was spent at home.[23]

---

comparison of the age of salvation with a wedding (Kittel, *The Theological Dictionary of the New Testament*, 1103), this is unlikely and inconsistent with the character of the Gospel.

20. Just, *Luke 1:1–9:50*, 248.
21. Argyle, *The Gospel according to Matthew*, 73.
22. Franzmann, *Follow me: Discipleship according to St. Matthew*, 77.
23. Barclay, *The Gospel of Matthew*, 335.

APPENDIX II

The best man, for instance, was an important wedding character. John the Baptist describes himself in such a relationship to Jesus in John 3:24, as the "friend of the bridegroom" (i.e. best man) who looks after the bride, takes care of arrangements, and prepares the way for the Bridegroom.[24] Accordingly, "for as long as bridegroom is with them" reflects the Jewish practice of extending wedding festivities for several days, or in other terms, Jesus' earthly ministry.[25]

Jesus uses the opportunity with John's disciples to speak not only of His identity but about His work as well, since the person and work of Christ as Messiah remain inseparable. Matthew's order of words and wording places the emphasis on the unity of Jesus' identity and work in a way that the other Gospels do not. The bridegroom is the subject in Matthew which is not the case for the Gospel according to St. Mark.[26] The bridegroom's immediate presence is even emphasized by the indication of a time when He will no longer be there[27] again highlighting the unity of His person and work.

Specifically, Jesus' work is to die. Jesus demonstrates His divinity and omnipotence by stating the fact that He will be "taken away", the first reference in the Gospel to Jesus suffering the violent crucifixion.[28] Then, "in those days", as the Latin text reads, they will fast often and frequently, in absence of their Lord, a prophecy similarly alluded to in Matthew 26:11. They will fast in sorrow and mourning. No-one will need to tell the disciples that they will have to fast when Jesus is taken from them! It will be the natural reaction. "When the heart is bowed down, fasting is a proper expression of its feelings. Who cares to eat at all, or more than a little, when he is greatly depressed?"[29]

The shadow of the cross darkens this moment of joyous teaching. Yet the cross always doubles as a symbol of hope. Because the figure of the Servant is ingrained in Christ's words and thought, the Christian cannot escape the disturbing yet beautiful truth that the love of the bridegroom is love of the Servant, selfless and sacrificing.[30] The text offers us a glimpse into the mystery of the two natures of Christ: our Lord belonging in the

24. Kittel, *The Theological Dictionary of the New Testament*, 1101.
25. Gundry, *Matthew: a Commentary on his Literary and Theological Art*, 170.
26. Ibid., 170.
27. Albright, *Matthew*, 35.
28. Tasker, *The Gospel according to St Matthew*, 98.
29. Lenski, *Interpretation of St. Matthew's Gospel*, 369.
30. Franzmann, *Follow me: Discipleship according to St. Matthew*, 77.

APPENDIX II

state of exaltation indicates His choice to suffer as a man in this state of humiliation.

Fasting and mourning are often notions that are used synonymously in the Old Testament. As mentioned above, fasting was done for a variety of reasons but mourning and repentance were the most common. This explains the later manuscript substitution of "mourn" with "fast". Similarly, the other Gospels do not say "mourn" but read "fast", probably to counter potential opinions that fasting was made obsolete by Jesus. Instead, Christians continued to fast after the resurrection but for different reasons.[31] The substitution of the terms, however, demonstrate that they are interchangeable notions.

With this in mind, is Jesus here referring to the time that the disciples would experience intense sorrow, until their tribulations turned to joy in the resurrection when they will once again cease to fast? In other words, is the time frame Jesus meant three days of grief, bitter weeping and sorrow, and likely abstinence from food?[32] Or is Jesus referring to the fasting that will occur by believers after Jesus dies and ascends? Because Christians universally continued to fast after His ascension, it appears that Jesus was not referring only to the time between His death and resurrection, but to the time of His absence from earth in His present form until His second coming. Incidentally the early believers fasted before the Eucharist, recognizing that during the Lord's Supper there is no need to fast since Christ is *really* with them. Likewise, the Desert Fathers and Benedictine monks would habitually break their fasts in the presence of a visitor, recognizing the presence of Christ in this stranger or alien. Fasting would take on an entirely different flavour amongst the Christians primarily because of these insights offered by our Lord. Christian fasting would become one of mourning and joy, corresponding to the 'already/not yet' eschatological understanding.

Christianity, unlike Judaism, is the religion of joy and 'the already', yet it also recognizes the 'not yet' aspect of being, explaining again for the early Church's fasting practices (which intentionally fasted on the days that the Jews did not, Wednesdays and Fridays in light of the Crucifixion, and before the Eucharist, although this became a somewhat later practice). Though some wonder whether or not we are saying greater things by not fasting at all, since Christ is ever present with us,[33] He is not ever present

---

31. Gundry, *Matthew: a Commentary on his Literary and Theological Art*, 169.
32. Tasker, *The Gospel according to St Matthew*, 98.
33. Argyle, *The Gospel according to Matthew*, 73.

APPENDIX II

with us *in the flesh* in a graspable way, which is why the Eucharistic fast is a strong confession in the real presence of the Lord in, with and under the consecrated elements of bread and wine in the Holy Communion. The Christian believes Christ to be present in this world according to different modes. The Christian fast is not something done in the absence of eschatological expectation. The Church as the bride fasts in joy and in sorrow; caught in the already/not yet tension[34] yet with her eyes on the heavenly supper to come,[35] offering an entirely new perspective of faith to the Jews who expected a political/worldly hero in the Messiah.

In this verse, Jesus not only predicts His future death and future fasting amongst His disciples, but also celebrates His real presence now in the midst of them. In Isaiah 58, fasting was a way of being heard by God and accessing His glory, but with Christ, there is no need, since He is already in their presence. His presence resembles the celebration of a wedding, not the mourning of a funeral (which will come in His death).[36] Jesus' compassionate presence among men made His days among them a time of rejoicing (4:16), hence His disciples were not typical of other religious people.[37] When one realizes who Jesus is, it is ridiculous to fast in His presence. One fasts in mourning and not during a wedding which is a time of joy! The motif of a wedding is tied to the preceding text on Jesus' table fellowship with sinners, a type of the Messianic banquet to come.[38] Sinners have no reason to feast, but only to fast. Yet this is not the case when you are a *forgiven* sinner who is a saint. And saints feast. Fellowship with Jesus means forgiveness of sins, a reason to feast and receive the new bread and new wine that He offers.[39]

Accordingly, Matthew juxtaposes Jesus with John. John's disciples lost their bridegroom to prison, giving them a reason to mourn.[40] In this sense, the Messianic Age is contrasted with the age of the Law, embodied in John and Jesus respectively. Fasting is the absence of table fellowship, and John is typological of this with his ascetic lifestyle[41] and a baptism of repentance.

34. Barclay, *The Gospel of Matthew*, 335.
35. Just, *Luke 1:1–9:50*, 248.
36. Gundry, *Matthew: a Commentary on his Literary and Theological Art*, 169.
37. Franzmann, *Follow me: Discipleship according to St. Matthew*, 77.
38. France, *Matthew*, 169.
39. Just, *Luke 1:1–9:50*, 249.
40. France, *Matthew*, 169.
41. Just, *Luke 1:1–9:50*, 248.

APPENDIX II

Jesus' disciples, in contrast, are not compelled to fast, signalling a new era of salvation,[42] a baptism of the Holy Spirit.

All this indicates that it is difficult to assert that Jesus condemns fasting except as an expression of real sorrow, as some argue,[43] but uses the question to unveil His true identity. Jesus claims to be the unique presence of God in the midst of man and is not interested in rules of fasting. On the contrary, in 6:17 we see that Jesus is indeed content with fasting for the correct reasons and motivations. However, Jesus alludes that the motivation to fast for His disciples will be entirely different than that of the Jews. The Christians will fast in a way that is totally different from that of the Jews, understood by the wine skin metaphor in the following verse.[44]

verse 16

Jesus turns His discourse to another example, demonstrating His authority and Messiahship but making a slightly different point. Once He establishes His identity alluding to His purpose, He goes on to comment on the meaning and implication of this work. Thus, the two parables make the same point: that Jesus as Messiah is the arrival of a new era of salvation.[45]

By the use of an individual saying of Jewish tradition, Jesus makes an expression of the universal. The image of the wineskin is used by Job: "Bottled up like wine, like new wineskins ready to burst" (Job 32:19). Fasting is a specific Jewish example of a universal truth. Jesus brings something

---

42. Ibid.

43. Tasker, *The Gospel according to St Matthew*, 98.

44. Lenski, *Interpretation of St. Matthew's Gospel*, 369. Jesus probably observed national fasts but not private ones after that, although He does not forbid them and presupposes voluntary fasts (Matt6:16ff). But the significance which He ascribes to fasting is wholly different from that which Judaism in fateful misunderstanding tends to associate with the custom. Fasting is the service of God. It is a sign and symbol of the conversion to God which takes place in concealment. Impressive displays before men defeats the end of true fasting. Fasting before God, the Father of those who turn to Him, is joy . . . Sorrow and fasting belong to the time of waiting for salvation. This is true for the disciples too, who by His death will be rudely put back in the state of waiting (Jn16:20). Seen from that standpoint of the Messianic eschatological centre of the message of Jesus, fasting is transcended. But since Jesus is aware of an interval between the Now and Then, between the dawn of salvation on earth and its consummation, He finds a place for fasting between the times (Kittel, The Theological Dictionary of the New Testament, 932-933).

45. Just, *Luke 1:1-9:50*, 248.

APPENDIX II

new and Judaism cannot contain it,[46] as already exemplified in the previous verse. The Jews were expecting a political hero in their Messiah, an end to all fasts and the beginning of all feasts of worldly victory, and yet Jesus promises more fasting and suffering. The text is really an instruction on the incompatibility of 'the new' that Jesus brings with 'the old' of Judaism. He breaks out of the confines of their legalism and asceticism[47] cleverly taught in a simple comparison:

> While the new wine was still fermenting, the gases gave off and put pressure on the skin. New skin has certain elasticity. The old lost its elasticity and did not give to the pressure of the gases and burst.[48]

Thus a patch was often used to fill in the tears. However, the patch carried away something from the old garment since the referred wineskin was a goatskin that was removed from the animal without slitting it; the openings at the feet and tail were bound up, leaving the neck as the mouth of the wineskin. The new skin stretches, but the old does not. Trying to preserve the old by attaching a little of the new makes it worse than before. One cannot patch Pharisaic Judaism with the new teaching of Jesus. He is not just another prophet. The baptism of Jesus replaces the baptism of John. One must discard the old robe of man's righteousness of the Law and take in its place the new robe of Christ's righteousness of the Gospel. The era of Grace has appeared in Christ Jesus and this era is by no means a continuation of the era of the Law,[49] thus the old covenant (testament) is placed in contradistinction with the new covenant (testament).

Hence, another way of saying this is that the messianic forgiveness cannot be contained in the wine-skins of Jewish legalism.[50] The new teaching of the Gospel cannot fit with old teaching of Judaism (or as Francis Pieper points out, the religion of the Gospel is radically different from all other religions, including Judaism, which are all religions of the Law). Jesus does not despise the Law/Old covenant/Judaism. He has not come to destroy the Law (Mat 5:17-20), because it has its place in the economy of salvation as it serves the Gospel (e.g. there is not absolution without confession). Yet

46. France, *Matthew*, 169.
47. France, *Matthew*, 169.
48. Barclay, *The Gospel of Matthew*, 335.
49. Lenski, *Interpretation of St. Matthew's Gospel*, 371.
50. Tasker, *The Gospel according to St Matthew*, 98.

APPENDIX II

intermixing the two results in the destruction of both. The 'old' is not kept by adding a *little* of the 'new' or combining *all* of it with it. In the new Messianic Age, the old plays a new role, but a somewhat different one. The current religious practices and teachings of Judaism as fostered by the Scribes and Pharisees became a religion which served itself leaving no room for the one which it had always awaited. In this sense, it collapsed upon itself when it stopped building itself upon Christ.[51] And although Christianity should have been welcomed by these Jews as an extension or fulfillment of Judaism, it became something despised, and a truly 'new' religion.

This new illustration also advances the same thought/principle of the one made in the preceding metaphor. The δέ relates the sayings of the wineskin and patches to the future fasting that Jesus foresees. Yet the motivation of the fasting will be different and 'new'[52] because the religion of the new Israel is different and new due to the coming of Jesus the Christ. The point is not that Jesus values new things for the sake of newness, as some have advocated in criticizing 'outdated' Christian theology. Jesus' teaching is not old today, but as new as ever[53] as we belong to the new covenant. Instead the idea is that the new and old covenants cannot be mixed.

verse 17

καινός (fresh) is the key term in this new eschatological promise,[54] and can be distinguished from νέος which is not an eschatological word. νέος refers to 'new' as "not existing before" and is bound to the notion of time in the New Testament. καινός (fresh) on the other hand, is 'new' over against 'old' or παλαιός which is bound to the notion of 'quality' in the New Testament. The new (καινός)(and better) era is filled by the new (νέος) (unheard of before) message and person of Christ.[55] Jesus does not merely offer new teachings but ushers in a new era! Hence, the text inculcates that both doctrines of Law and Gospel are 'preserved' in this way[56] and should not be intermingled or confused. Christ is therefore not saying that both Law and Gospel must be preserved in that allegiance to John or Jesus, Judaism or

---

51. Argyle, *The Gospel according to Matthew*, 73.
52. Gundry, *Matthew: a Commentary on his Literary and Theological Art*, 170.
53. Lenski, *Interpretation of St. Matthew's Gospel*, 371.
54. Just, *Luke 1:1—9:50*, 249.
55. Ibid.
56. Lenski, *Interpretation of St. Matthew's Gospel*, 371.

APPENDIX II

Christianity are equally valid[57] as some suggest. Both Law and Gospel are needed and confusing them spoils them both. Thus, an alternate reading drives this point that not properly distinguishing between the two results in the complete destruction of both. "The wine in the skins of this one *will burst*" omitting "and the wine *is spilled*".

Unlike Mark and Luke who emphasize the *wine*, Matthew places the *wineskins* as the subject of verb so that he can easily assert by the independent clause that either both are preserved, or both perish.[58] Thus Matthew is unique with "and both are preserved". St. Luke states that "no one after drinking old wine desires new; for he says, 'the old is good'". Matthew again, stressing Christ's fulfillment of Judaism, does not want to be interpreted by the Jews as advocating a jettison of the old (i.e. Christ was not an inventor of a new religion), but wants to restore it to its proper place in the economy of salvation. Although St. Luke's Gospel with its less Jewish flavour is clearest with the freshness of the Gospel which is new in time and new in nature (e.g. he repeats "fresh" three times), Matthew is more cautious in using this radical language which could be misunderstood and interpreted to mean Christianity is a sectarian Jewish group [Rom 9-11 shows concern felt about precise relationship of the Messianic community to Judaism[59]]. Matthew desires to make clear that Christ is the *fulfiller* of the Law, and not its destroyer. The "fullness" of Christ cannot be contained by the restrictions of Judaism, which is "unfulfilled" cloth (πληρόω is "to fulfill" and Christ "fulfills" the demands of the Law).

Although the Christian casts aside old Pharisaism with all its ways and takes instead a new way/ethos of life in accordance with the new doctrine, the old way is still necessary in guiding us to the new way. Even the word "preservation" strengthens Matthew's stress on the coming of Jesus to fulfill the law and prophets rather than destroy them (chapter 5).[60] In Lutheran language, the old is required in order to hold onto the new since the Law acts as a mirror to lead us to the Gospel. After all, Judaism is Christianity's inheritance. It is not a past phenomenon external to it, but a continuing presence carried on within it.[61]

57. Albright, *Matthew*, 108.
58. Gundry, *Matthew: a Commentary on his Literary and Theological Art*, 171.
59. Albright, *Matthew*, 36.
60. Gundry, *Matthew: a Commentary on his Literary and Theological Art*, 171.
61. Davies, *St. Matthew*, 112. The practices are preserved as well, yet with new meaning, validating Christian worship as a continuation of that encountered in the synagogue,

APPENDIX II

These words of Jesus function also as an indirect prophecy to God's people. The newness of Jesus will cause division amongst the people of God. As stated earlier, one must see the wedding, garment, wine, etc., all as eschatological symbols as they relate to Jewish theology. The "tearing away" or "schisma" acts as a metaphor for this separation as well.[62] The Jewish religion will split as the old embraces the Law and despises this Gospel (Rom 7:6). The Law comes through Moses (and John![63]), but grace comes through Jesus Christ (John 1:17).

Central Thought

Jesus the Messiah, God made flesh to save the world, predicts the day of sorrow, when the Bridegroom will die on the cross and when fasting will once again be appropriate. Yet while God is present, there is no need to fast, but rather to celebrate and feast. Yet even in Jesus' absence after His Ascension into heaven and when His children will once again fast, this work of piety will take on a different character since what Jesus brings is new. Because He is the fulfiller of the Law, all the practices of His people are driven by the Gospel and done out of joy and in the freedom that He gives.

Summary and Application

Although we should fast today for a variety of reasons, we need to remember that we fast for different ones than that of the Jews of old. Matthew teaches us that we are children of the new era, and that we ought to fast in sorrow and joy, out of love and devotion and not in order to earn God's favour. We remember in the Litany that by Jesus' birth, fasting, death and

---

and Christian observances and piety as similar to that of the Jews. So, too, with fasting. Christians fast but they do not fast like the Jews, but rather in the newness brought by Christ. Christians do not fast in an attempt to fulfill the Law but out of a thankful heart.

62. The middle and passive form of several verbs in verses 16 and 17 convey the idea of the inevitability of the consequence. Yet the two consequences are contrasted with one another again emphasizing the incompatibility of the old and new (Moses and Christ) and the inevitable destruction of both when they are united.

63. As said above, John's asceticism is contrasted with Jesus' celebration; John announces sombre repentance, Jesus announces good news (Davies, *St Matthew*, 109). Yet typologically even John characterizes or embodies 'repentance', where Christ embodies 'forgiveness'. Hence one could argue that in John and Jesus we have enfleshed both doctrines of Law and Gospel.

APPENDIX II

Resurrection, He has redeemed us. Jesus is the ultimate faster who fasted for our sake, perfecting all of our imperfect fasts.

And, so, St. Irenaeus said that Jesus fasted in order to give the devil an area to attack Him, so He could conquer Him once and for all. Unlike Adam, who was not hungry yet filled himself with the forbidden food and sinned, Jesus who was hungry waited for God's nourishment.[64] The Israelites who were not hungry tested God in the desert; Jesus who was hungry refused to test His father in the desert.[65] Jesus' refusal of nourishment is no mere ascetic exercise, as one who has been apprehended by the spirit (Matt 4:1; Luke 4:1). He lives in a world where different conditions of life apply from those of earth. He fasted for our sake and has made all of our fasts beautiful works before God.

Because of Jesus' fast, our fasts are ones of joy. Fasting is a sign and symbol of the conversion to God. Impressive displays before men defeat the end of true fasting. Fasting before God, the Father of those who turn to Him, is joy. Sorrow and fasting belong to the time of waiting for salvation. This is true for the disciples too, who by His death were rudely put back in the state of waiting (John 16:20). Seen from that standpoint of the Messianic eschatological centre of the message of Jesus, fasting is transcended. But since Jesus is aware of an interval between Now and Then, between the dawn of salvation on earth and its consummation, He finds a place for fasting between the times. It is not of course a pious work.[66] It is a sign and symbol of the inner attitude which perhaps hardly needs such a sign and symbol. The attitude of Jesus to fasting is not unlike that of the prophets. But the reasons and concrete expression are His own, uniquely determined by His Messianic consciousness.[67]

Yet Jesus in the passage does not only teach us about the new shape of God's people's thoughts and lives because of His death and in His absence, He also teaches us something about His presence passed along to us through tradition. The Jews banned fasting during the Passover and other 'Christological' festivals[68] to prepare God's people for the time when the bridegroom is with us and when we ought not to fast, but rather feast and

---

64. Wimmer, *Fasting in the New Testament*, 31.
65. Ibid., 43.
66. Kittel, *The Theological Dictionary of the New Testament*, 932.
67. Ibid., 933.
68. Block, *The Biblical and Historical background of Jewish Customs and Ceremonies*, 298.

eat with the Lord. For Christ teaches us that it is nonsensical to fast while He is in our midst, but rather *that* is a time to eat and celebrate. When else is He more in our midst than in the celebration of the Holy Supper?

The Bridegroom calls those who are labouring in the body to eat. Those who have set aside their bodies He calls to drink, no longer feeding on the bread of sorrow (Ps 126:2) but the bread of life.[69]

---

69. Bernard of Clairvaux. *Selected Works*, 198.

APPENDIX III

Fasting and the Word: A Bible Study

How does fasting fit into the words of Paul in 1 Corinthians 9:24-27? How does our baptism fit in?

How does fasting relate to spiritual warfare? See Matthew 17:21 and Mark 9:29 (in some Bibles) for help. Read (or sing) the words of the old hymn, "Onward Christians Soldiers". How are other Christian activities part of spiritual warfare?

How is the main purpose of fasting found in the words of Deuteronomy 8:3 and Psalm 51:16-17?

How does fasting visually proclaim the Law and the Gospel at the same time? How may Romans 5:20 help? Now fix your eyes upon a crucifix and ask the question again.

How does fasting reveal what is important to us? What sort of things do you feel you could not survive without? *How* could you fast from these things for a while? *Why* should you fast from these things for a while?

According to Isaiah 58:3-7 what is a 'true' fast? What was the error of the Israelites? How is the message in Zechariah 7:4-10 similar?

What is Jesus' point in Matthew 6:16-18? Is He addressing *our attitude* while fasting or is He instructing us to always keep our fasts hidden (i.e.

APPENDIX III

never letting others know that we are fasting)? How does 6:1-15 answer our question?

When looking at Matthew 6:1-18 and Isaiah 58:3-7 what sort of relationship exists between prayer, fasting and good works/almsgiving?

How does *suffering* fit into this relationship? See Psalm 51:16-17 and Psalm 35:13-14 for help.

How is fasting an expression of sorrow? See 1 Sam 28:20. How is prayer an expression of weakness? Would you agree or disagree with this statement: Christians are always fasting; Christians are always praying. Why or why not?

"Fasting is the package of the prayer". Comment.

Is it okay to fast for specific things and over specific concerns? See Ezra 8:21-23; Esther 4:6-16. How can this kind of fasting be dangerous to our faith (i.e. by attempting to get what *we* want from God)? Does fasting change God or does it change us?

Why should we fast as a Church as well as individuals? See Jonah 3:4-10, Joel 2:12, 1 Samuel 7:6.

In Luke 2:36-38 we hear about Anna the prophetess who fasted and prayed day and night. She certainly ate meals and slept sometimes, so she wasn't literally fasting and praying ALL the time, yet she was characterized in this way by others. How are Christians characterized by the world (good and bad)? How are we witnesses of the Gospel even when we are characterized in a bad way? How is this good news?

How do we serve our neighbour in fasting? How does this quote from Luther capture the spirit of Lent?: "If men desire to maintain a brotherhood, they should gather a table full of poor people, for the sake of God, the day before they should fast, and on the feast day remain sober, passing the time in prayer and other good works."

APPENDIX III

Reflect on these words: "my own anguish calls forth the anguish of others. It reminds them of their own emptiness and isolation". Could we say that fasting is evangelism?

Why should we fast before Holy Communion? Reflect upon the following passages: Jeremiah 36:1-9; Deut 9:9/Exodus 34:28; Mt 9:14-17. Why do you think it is appropriate to fast in the presence of God (wherever we may encounter Him)? When we fast before Holy Communion, what are we proclaiming to the unbelieving world and also those Christians who don't take Holy Communion seriously? What can we learn from some fasting monks who would break their fasts in the presence of a visitor? How then can fasting change the way *we* view other people?

If someone said to you "fasting is nonsense. I don't need to fast," what would you say?

In the Litany we speak how Jesus fasted in the wilderness for us. How does Matthew 4:1-11 help us to put *our* fasting and all of our good deeds, prayers for others, and pious activities in perspective? Read (or sing) Hymn 418 in LSB "O Lord, Throughout these Forty Days" and say a prayer to Jesus in your own words.

"I feel there are especially necessary for me in this life two things without which its miseries would be unbearable. Confined here in this prison of the body I confess I need these two, food and light. Therefore, You [O Jesus] have given me in my weakness Your sacred Flesh to refresh my soul and body, and You have set Your Word as the guiding light for my feet. Without them I could not live aright, for the Word of God is the light of my soul and Your Sacrament is the Bread of Life.

These also may be called the two tables, one here, one there, in the treasure house of the holy Church. One is the table of the holy altar, having the holy Bread that is the precious Body of Christ. The other is the table of divine law, containing holy doctrine that teaches all the true faith and firmly leads them within the veil, the Holy of Holies.

Thanks to You, Creator and Redeemer of men, who, to declare Your love to all the world, have prepared a great supper in which You have placed before us as food not the lamb, the type of Yourself, but Your own most precious Body and Blood, making all the faithful glad in Your sacred banquet, intoxicating them with the chalice of salvation in which are all the delights of paradise; and the holy angels feast with us but with more happiness and sweetness."

THOMAS À KEMPIS, THE IMITATION OF CHRIST IV.3

BIBLIOGRAPHY

Adalbert de Vogüé. *The Rule of Saint Benedict: Doctrinal and Spiritual Commentary.* Michigan: Cistercians Publications, 1983.
Albright, William Foxwell. *Matthew.* The Anchor Bible. New York: Doubleday, 1971.
Ambrose. *Letters. The Fathers of the Church 26.* Washington D.C.: The Catholic University of America Press, 1954.
Anglin, Thomas Francis. *The Eucharistic Fast.* Washington D.C.: The Catholic University of America Press, 1941.
Argyle, A.W. *The Gospel according to Matthew.* The Cambridge Bible Commentary. London: Cambridge University Press, 1963.
Arndt, Johann. *True Christianity.* Toronto: Paulist, 1979.
Augustine. "Sermons for Christmas and Epiphany". *Ancient Christian Writers* 15. New York: Newman, 1948.
———. "Sermons on Liturgical Seasons". *Fathers of the Church* 38. Washington D.C.: The Catholic University of America Press, 1959.
Barclay, William. *The Gospel of Matthew.* Philadelphia: Westminster, 1975.
Berghuis, Kent D. "A Biblical Perspective on Fasting". *Bibliotheca Sacra* 158 (January-March 2001) 86–103.
Bernard of Clairvaux. *Selected Works.* New York: Paulist, 1987.
Berry, Paul. *Fasting Safely.* California: Word Publications, 1982.
Bloch, Abraham. *The Biblical and Historical background of Jewish Customs and Ceremonies.* New York: Ktav Publishing, 1980.
Braaten, Carl. And LaVonne. *The Living Temple: A practical Theology of the Body and the Foods of the earth.* New York: Harper and Row, 1976.
Brattston, David W.T. "Fasting in the Earliest Church". *Restoration Quarterly* 53:4 (2011) 235–245.
Braulio of Saragosa. *Writings.* Fathers of the Church. Washington D.C.: The Catholic University Press of America, 1969.
Brown, Francis; Driver, C.R.; Briggs, Charles. *Hebrew and English Lexicon of the Old Testament.* Oxford: Clarendon, 1975.
Buksbazen, Victor. *The Gospel in the Feasts of Israel.* Philadelphia: Continental, 1954.
Buttrick, Arthur G. *The Book of Isaiah.* The Interpreter's Bible V. New York: Abingdon, 1939.
Catharine of Siena. *The Dialogue.* New York: Paulist, 1980.

BIBLIOGRAPHY

Caesarius of Arles. "Sermons." *Fathers of the Church* 66. Washington D.C.: The Catholic University Press of America, 1973.
Campbell, Peter A; Edwin M. McMahon. *Bio-Spirituality: Focusing as a Way to Grow.* Chicago: Loyola University Press, 1985.
Cassiodorus. *Explanation of Psalm 52*. Ancient Christian Writers. New York: Paulist, 1991.
Chemnitz, Martin. *Examination of the Council of Trent (Part II)*. St. Louis: CPH, 1978.
———. *Examination of the Council of Trent (Part IV)*. St. Louis: CPH, 1986.
Chrysologus, Peter. *Sermons*. Fathers of the Church. Washington D.C.: The Catholic University Press of America, 1953.
Chrysostom, John. *Baptismal Instructions*. Ancient Christian Writers 31. New York: Newman, 1963.
———. "Discourses against Judaizing Christians". *Fathers of the Church* 68, Washington D.C.: The Catholic University Press of America, 1979.
Cyprian, *The Lapsed*. Ancient Christian Writers 25. New York: Newman, 1956.
Cyril of Jerusalem. *Works*. Fathers of the Church 1. Washington D.C.: The Catholic University Press of America, 1969.
Davidson, Benjamin. *The Analytical Hebrew and Chaldee Lexicon*. Grand Rapids: Zondervan, 1980.
Davies, W.D. and Allison, Pale. *St Matthew*. The International Critical Commentary 1. Edinburgh: T and T Clark, 1991.
Deinzer, Johann. *Wilhelm Löhe's Leben II*. Güttersloh: C. Bertelsmann, 1880.
Delitzsch, Franz and Keil. *The Prophecies of Isaiah III*. Michigan: William B. Eerdmans Publishing Co., 1965.
The Didache. Ancient Christian Writers 6, New York: Paulist, 1948.
Elliger, K and Rudolph, W. *Biblia Hebraica Stuttgartensia*. Stuttgart: Deutsche Bibelgesellschaft, 1967.
Elliott, John H. *The Christ Life*. Chicago: Walther League, 1968.
Foster, Richard. *Celebration of Discipline*. New York: Harper and Row, 1978.
France, R.T. *Matthew*. Tyndale New Testament Commentaries. Michigan: Eerdman's, 1985.
Franzmann, Martin H. *Follow me: Discipleship according to St. Matthew*. Saint Louis: CPH, 1961.
———. *The Word of the Lord Grows*. Saint Louis: CPH, 1961.
Freedman, David Noel. *The Anchor Bible Dictionary*. New York: Doubleday, 1992.
———. *Isaiah II*. *The Anchor Bible Dictionary*. New York: Doubleday, 1992.
Gillet, Archimandrite Lev. *The Jesus Prayer*. New York: St. Vladimir's Seminary Press, 1997.
Gundry, Robert. *Matthew: a Commentary on his Literary and Theological Art*. Grand Rapids: Eerdmans, 1982.
Grothe, Jonathon. *Reclaiming Patterns of Pastoral Ministry: Jesus and Paul*. St. Louis: CPH, 1988.
Herbert, A.J. *Isaiah 40–66*. The Cambridge Bible Commentary. Cambridge: Cambridge University Press, 1975.
Hoerber, Robert (ed). *Concordia Self Study Bible. New International Version*. St. Louis: CPH. 1986.
Holladay, William L. (ed). *A Concise Hebrew and Aramaic Lexicon of the Old Testament*. Grand Rapids: Eerdmans, 1988.
Hummel, Horace. *The Word Becoming Flesh*. St. Louis: CPH, 1979.

BIBLIOGRAPHY

Hunter, David (ed.). *Preaching in the Patristic Age*. New York: Paulist, 1989.
Iberian Fathers. "Sayings of the Egyptian Fathers." *Fathers of the Church* 62. Washington D.C.: The Catholic University Press of America, 1969.
Jerome. *Letters*. Ancient Christian Writers 33. New York: Newman: 1963.
———. *Homilies*. Fathers of the Church. Washington D.C.: The CatholicUniversity Press of America, 1966.
John of the Cross. *Selected Writings*. New York: Paulist, 1987.
Jones, Cheslyn; Wainwright, Geoffrey; Yarnold, Edward. *The Study of Spirituality*. Oxford: Oxford University Press, 1986.
Just, Arthur A. *Luke 1:1–9:50*. Concordia Commentary. Saint Louis: CPH, 1996.
Kelley, Page. *Biblical Hebrew: An Introductory Grammar*. Grand Rapids: Eerdmans, 1992.
Kingsbury, Jack Dean. *Matthew as Story*. Philadelphia: Fortress, 1986.
Kittel, Gerhard. *The Theological Dictionary of the New Testament IV*. Grand Rapids: Eerdmans, 1967.
Knobel, Peter S. *Jewish Fasts: Gates of the Seasons*. New York: Central Conference of American Rabbis, 1983.
Koehler, Ludwig, and Baumgartner, Walter. *Hebrew and Aramaic Lexicon of the Old Testament III*. Leiden: E.J. Brill, 1996.
Koehler, Walter. *Counseling and Confession: The Role of Confession and Absolution in Pastoral Counselling*. St. Louis: CPH, 1982.
Kolb, Erwin. *Jewish Holidays*. St. Louis: LCMS, 1987.
Lambert, David. "Fasting as a Penitential Rite: A Biblical Phenomenon?". *Harvard Theological Review* 96:4 (2003) 477–512.
Larin, Vassa. "Feasting and Fasting According to the Byzantine Typikon". *Worship*. 83:2 (March 2009) 133–148.
Lenski, R.C.H. *Interpretation of St. Matthew's Gospel*. Minneapolis: Augsburg, 1943.
Leupold, H.C. *Exposition of Isaiah II*. Grand Rapids: Baker, 1971.
Löhe, Willhelm. *On Mercy: Six Chapters for Everyone, the Seventh for the Servants of Mercy*. St. Louis: LCMS, 2015.
Loughlin, Stephen. "Thomas Aquinas and the importance of fasting to the Christian life". *PRO ECCLESIA* XVII:3 (2008) 343–361.
Luther, Martin. *Luther's Works*. St. Louis: CPH/Augsburg, 1959.
Lutheran Worship. St. Louis: CPH, 1982.
Maximus of Turin. *Sermons*. Ancient Christian Writers 50. New York: Newman, 1989.
McKenzie, Joel L. *Second Isaiah*. The Anchor Bible. New York: Doubleday, 1968.
Metzger, Bruce M., and Murphy E. Roland (ed). *The New Oxford Annotated Bible* (NRSV). New York: Oxford University Press, 1994.
New American Standard Bible. Nashville: Broadman and Hollman Publishers, 1977.
New Catholic Encyclopedia. New York: McGraw-Hill, 1967.
Nouen, Henri J.M. *Heart Speaks to heart: 3 prayers to Jesus*. Indiana: Ave Maria, 1989.
Palladius. *The Lausiac history*. Ancient Christian Writers 34. New York: Newman, 1964.
Papathanassiou, Athanasios H. "Christian Fasting in Postmodern Society: Considering the Criteria." *St. Vladimir's Theological Quarterly* 60:1–2 (2016) 249–268.
Patrick. *Ancient Christian Writers* 17. New York: Newman, 1963.
Paulinus of Nola. *Letters*. Ancient Christian Writers 36. New York: Newman, 1967.
Pelikan, Jarsolav. *The Growth of Medieval Theology (600–1300)*. Chicago: University of Chicago Press,1978.

BIBLIOGRAPHY

———. *The Illustrated Jesus Through the Centuries*. New Haven: Yale University Press, 1997.

Julianus Pomerius. *Ancient Christian writers* 4. New York: Newmann, 1947.

Reijnen, Anne Marie. "Fasting – Some Protestant Remarks on 'Not by Bread Alone': An Argument for the Contemporary Value of Christian Fasting. *St. Vladimir's Theological Quarterly*. 60:1–2 (2016) 269–278.

Ruddy, James. *The Apostolic Constitution: Christus Dominus*. Washington, D.C.: The Catholic University of America Press, 1957.

Russell, Norman. *The Lives of the Desert Fathers*. London: Mowbray, 1981.

Schouss, Hayyim. *Guide to Jewish Holy days*. New York: Union of American Hebrew Congregations, 1962.

Schroeder, John E. *Skip-a-meal Meditations*. St. Louis: Board of Social Ministry and World Relief of LCMS, 1980.

Sullivan, Jordan. *Fast and Abstinence in the First order of St. Francis: a historical synopsis and commentary*. Washington: Catholic university of American Press, 1957.

Swanson, Reuben J. *The Horizontal Line Synopsis of the Gospels*. Dillsboro: Western North Carolina, 1975.

Symeon the New Theologian. *The Discourses*. Toronto: Paulist, 1980.

Tasker, R.V.G. *The Gospel according to St Matthew*. Tyndale New Testament Commentaries. Grand Rapids: Eerdmans, 1978.

Tertullian. "Treatise on Marriage and Remarriage". *Ancient Christian Writers* 13. New York: Newman, 1951.

———. "Treatise on Penance". *Ancient Christian Writers* 28, New York: Newman Press, 1959.

Towns, Elmer L. *Fasting for Spiritual Breakthrough: A guide to 9 biblical fasts*. California: Thomas Nelson, 1996.

Waddell, Helen. *The Desert Fathers*. Michigan: The University of Michigan Press, 1972.

Walther, C.F.W. *The Proper Distinction Between Law and Gospel*. Saint Louis: CPH, 1986.

Westerman, Claus. *Isaiah 40–66: A Commentary*. Philadelphia: The Westminister Press, 1969.

Wimmer, Joseph F. *Fasting in the New Testament*. Toronto: Paulist, 1982.

Witherspoon, Alexander M., and Warnke, Frank J. *Seventeenth-Century Prose and Poetry*. London: Harcourt Brace Jovanovich College, 1982.

Witetschek, Stephan. "Going Hungry for a Purpose: On the Gospel of Thomas 69.2 and a Neglected Parallel in Origin". *JSNT* 32:4 (2010) 379–393.

Yee, Gale. *Jewish Feasts and the Gospel of John*. Delaware: Michael Glazier, 1989.

Young, Edward. *The Book of Isaiah vol III*. Grand Rapids: W.B. Eerdmans, 1972.

Zodhiates, Spiros (ed). *The Hebrew-Greek Key Study Bible: King James Version*. Chattanooga: AMG, 1991.

www.ingramcontent.com/pod-product-compliance
Lightning Source LLC
Chambersburg PA
CBHW072134160426
43197CB00012B/2099